Sofia and children meditate on The Grain of Wheat at Via degli Orsini

CATECHESIS OF THE GOOD SHEPHERD

ESSENTIAL REALITIES

CATECHESIS OF THE GOOD SHEPHERD

ESSENTIAL REALITIES

Edited by Tina Lillig

**Catechesis of
the Good Shepherd
Publications**

CATECHESIS OF THE GOOD SHEPHERD: ESSENTIAL REALITIES © 2004 Archdiocese of Chicago: Liturgy Training Publications, 1800 North Hermitage Avenue, Chicago IL 60622-1101; 1-800-933-1800, fax 1-800-933-7094, e-mail orders@ltp.org. All rights reserved. See our website at www.ltp.org.

Catechesis of the Good Shepherd Publications is an imprint of Liturgy Training Publications (LTP). Further information about these publications is available from LTP or from the Catechesis of the Good Shepherd, PO Box 1084, Oak Park IL 60304; 708-524-1210; fax 708-386-8032. Requests for information about other aspects of the Catechesis should be directed to this address.

This book was edited by Tina Lillig. Carol Mycio was the production editor. The design is by M. Urgo, and the typesetting was done by Jim Mellody-Pizzato in Times and Bembo. The cover photo is from Scala/Art Resource N.Y., *The Good Shepherd*, Musei Vaticani. The art itself is a statue of the Good Shepherd from 200 AD, now in the Vatican Museums in Rome. A replica of this statue can be found in every atrium of the Catechesis of the Good Shepherd.

Printed in Canada.

Library of Congress Control Number: 2004109865

ISBN 1-56854-558-4
CGSER

Contents

Introduction   ix
    Tina Lillig

The Adventure of the Catechesis   1
    Rebekah Rojcewicz

Catechesis as Celebration   8
    Dalmazio Mongillo, OP

With Prayer We Speak to God   13
    Silvana Quattrocchi Montanaro, MD

An Opening into the Way of Love   17
    Luigi Capogrossi

Memories of Forty Years in the Atrium   23
    Patrizia Cocchini

Memories of "a Big Girl Who Helps Sofia"   30
    Francesca Cocchini

I Leave My Heart Here   36
    Patricia Coulter

Gianna   46
    Sofia Cavalletti

Mysterious Growth   51
    Tina Lillig

Familiar Faces and Places (photos)   63

A History of Growth in Joy   73
    Lupita Palafox

A Transforming Moment: Kingdom Song   78
    Ignatius Feaver, OFM CAP

Modern Montessori in Search of a Soul   80
    David Kahn

The Secure Child:
Attachment and Emotional Development in the Atrium   88
    Barbara Schmich Searle

The Child: A Scriptural Image of the Holy Spirit   102
    Francesca Cocchini

Reflections of Some Former Children of Sofia's and Gianna's Atrium   107

Contributors   114

Introduction

How does a book come to be? A word is spoken, curiosity awakened, a desire born. Then there is usually a time of waiting. The effort required for any book calls for an opportune moment or a worthy occasion in order to gather the energy for such a project.

The volume of essays we are presenting had an additional impetus: a profound thanksgiving. Those involved in the Catechesis of the Good Shepherd are an international community of adults and children who gather, usually in their churches or schools, to reflect on biblical and liturgical themes. Their joy is well expressed in the words of Jesus, which one author cited, in part, at the beginning of her essay: "I thank you, Father, Lord of heaven and earth, because you have hidden these things from the wise and the intelligent and revealed them to infants; yes, Father, for such was your gracious will" (Luke 10:21).

Over a decade ago, catechist Carol Nyberg introduced me to a new word: *festschrift*. It is a German word, and was strange to my ears and full of mystery. She explained that it means "celebration writing" and consists of a book-length collection of essays, usually published on the occasion of an academic milestone. Could we bring about a *festschrift* to celebrate the Catechesis of the Good Shepherd?

In the year 2000, we marked the twenty-fifth anniversary of Catechesis of the Good Shepherd in the United States and, at the time, the *festschrift* idea barely crossed my mind. But a new thought entered: When the catechists of our generation are gathered, how easy it is to recall how the Catechesis of the Good Shepherd began and grew in our country! But we know so little about its first two decades. What was it like when Sofia Cavalletti and Gianna Gobbi began to use this approach to the religious formation of children? How did it change and evolve into what it is today? Who were the people who joined them and supported them? What impact did the Second Vatican Council have on their work? How did it spread to so many countries? What are the little stories that would help us know more about the beginning days of this work?

So we started to speak, in casual conversation, about a "celebration volume" to mark the fiftieth anniversary of the Catechesis of the Good Shepherd in 2004. With Sofia's help we decided to focus on the Catechesis itself. We chose a working title and wrote acquisition letters. Enthusiastic responses came back immediately, and it was only then that we discovered another essential element for this book: it was waiting to be written.

For some readers, this volume will be a first introduction to the Catechesis of the Good Shepherd. "What exactly is it?" they may ask. As you read through this collection, you will find that several writings help to answer that question: the "memories" essay of Francesca Cocchini, Patricia Coulter's reflections, and in particular Tina Lillig's essay and the compiled reflections of former atrium children. But for now, I'll briefly explain three terms that appear in the opening pages:

1. *Via degli Orsini*—the street in Rome, near *Piazza Navona,* where Sofia lives. Her home is also the home of the Catechesis, *Centro di Catechesi,* consisting of the rooms where the children and adults meet.

2. Atrium (pl. atria)—a room that has been carefully prepared for the children. There are tables and chairs, appropriate to the size of the children who will come, and well-ordered shelves for the handmade catechetical materials that the children will use.

3. The Good Shepherd—the image of Jesus that is offered to the youngest children and from which this catechesis takes its name. We have seen the children come to love Jesus, their Good Shepherd, and continue to refer to him and address him in this way throughout their lives.

We are blessed to have a great diversity of contributors to this collection. Some are experts in the fields of law, medicine, education, psychology, or theology. Some wrote from the perspective of a mother, a father, or a catechist. Sofia herself tells us treasured stories of Gianna, her close collaborator. Half of the writers were there in the beginning years and their memories are like a window through which we can look, a door that opens to us, inviting us to be at home in a work we are drawn to. We will sense the slow pace of this work and the social networks that brought it about. We will even learn some nicknames!

In the first essay, Rebekah Rojcewicz, an American catechist, brings us to Sofia's house in Rome. She tells us about her years there as a student of Sofia and then describes their recent conversations about the beginnings, the development, and the future of the Catechesis of the Good Shepherd.

The next five essays are written by those who were close collaborators and participants in the work of Sofia and Gianna, beginning in the 1950s and '60s. As we read the piece by Father Dalmazio Mongillo, we may find ourselves pausing after almost every sentence. He offers such a profound and yet utterly simple understanding of the catechesis of young children that invites us into "the community that is joined together in the Shepherd." Silvana Quattrocchi Montanaro's essay introduces us to a network of amazing young women living in Rome in the 1950s. As a mother and physician, she describes how she was led by a Montessori "assistant to infancy," by a philosophy professor/Montessorian, and by her own little daughter to undertake biblical and Montessori studies and to work with adolescents in the atrium at Via degli Orsini.

Luigi Capogrossi recounts the birth of the Maria Montessori Association for the Religious Formation of the Child. He does so with affection, sharing his impressions of the personalities of its two founding mothers and the impact their work has had on his own life. The next two writings are by Patrizia Cocchini, a physician, and Francesca Cocchini, a professor of the history of early Christianity. They share many personal stories of growing up in the atrium, from child to adolescent to adult. Their words convey the intimacy of the atrium and the beautiful realities discovered there.

For over 20 years, Sofia and Gianna welcomed adult students from around the world to come to Rome for a two- or three-year course in this Montessori approach to the religious formation of children. Patricia Coulter, a Canadian catechist, describes in her essay what it was like to be one of those students.

Then, in the middle of the book, Sofia writes about Gianna, and in these precious pages we are introduced to Gianna as Sofia knew her. We read about life at Gianna's country house and its rhythm of work and rest; we see, with new eyes, the substance of the atrium: the essential, the real, and the natural.

The next two essays by Tina Lillig and Lupita Palafox are about the "reception" of the Catechesis of the Good Shepherd in the two countries where its growth has been surprisingly rapid—the United States and Mexico. A Franciscan brother from Canada who participated in a course given by Sofia in Houston shares how adults can be as affected by this catechesis as children.

The next three chapters, 12 to 14, are significant because they offer us something new: the emergence of reflections on the Catechesis of the Good Shepherd from the perspectives of related disciplines. With its history of 50 years and its presence in numerous countries, the Catechesis of the Good

Shepherd enjoys a grounded position from which to invite these reflections that both enrich and honor it. Each of the three authors in this section has an ongoing connection with the work of an atrium. David Kahn, a lifelong leader of the Montessori movement in North America, clarifies the early vision of Maria Montessori and the particular contribution of the Catechesis of the Good Shepherd in responding to the child's spiritual needs. Barbara Schmich Searle, a psychologist who is also a catechist and mother, offers us research on the infant and young child from the field of psychology. This is an area of great interest to catechists of children, and Barbara invites an attentiveness and sensitivity toward infants that will continue to form and assist the adult catechist. Francesca Cocchini shares her research and reflection on Origen's interpretation of a familiar passage from the Gospel of Matthew. Through her words on the dignity of the "child" to which Jesus refers, we are helped to begin to grasp all the dedication, care, energy, and joy of the past 50 years that is revealed in the pages of this book.

As a conclusion, the last section is written by the children, the *ex-bambini* of Sofia's and Gianna's atrium, grown up now and still discovering the "pearl," still aware of the presence of the Shepherd.

Over 40 persons, from several countries, had a hand in this book. Heartfelt thanks to the *"festschrift* team" of Patricia Coulter, Suzanne Lewis, and Donna Turner. Patricia and Suzanne were there in the early stages of the project, Patricia drafting letters to authors and Suzanne meeting with me to consider titles and contributors and later editing my editing. Donna rescued us with her encouragement and her keyboarding skills. Sofia Cavalletti and Rebekah Rojcewicz were our wise and gentle advisers, and Margaret Brennan, from Liturgy Training Publications, guided us along each step of the project. Inexpressible gratitude goes to the translators: Maureen Armas, Patricia Coulter, Kathy Dahl-Bredine, Patricia Huse, Father Joseph Occhio, and Rebekah Rojcewicz. Their careful work preserved the cultural and linguistic flavor of each piece of writing. Without them we truly would not have this volume.

And, of course, the children, both little and grown up, who are part of this 50-year history, have been our greatest inspiration. We are thankful that they continue to instruct us in the Catechesis of the Good Shepherd.

Tina Lillig

The Adventure of the Catechesis

Rebekah Rojcewicz

Once again I am amazed and very grateful to be back at Via degli Orsini. Even my first time here, when I came to do a two-year course of study in the Catechesis of the Good Shepherd in 1979, had felt like a homecoming. "You prepare a table before me. . . ." It was as if my place had been set at this table forever, awaiting my arrival. Here I heard my own name being called again and was able to lie down in a pasture that was more beautiful than I could have asked for or imagined. Here, unlike in any previous university experience, or even in my experience of Montessori training, I felt respected and loved, as the children are. I experienced the freedom to "just be," to contemplate and enjoy the pearl I had known since childhood but had mislaid in early adulthood.

This time back it is summer, the first time I've ever been in Rome in the summer, and it is hot. My fellow catechist and traveling companion, Donna Turner, and I spent our first night here in a *pensione* nearby, one that was familiar to me from previous visits. But those visits were never in summer; thus, the lack of air conditioning had never mattered before. In the wee hours of the morning, having had no sleep because of the heat and the traffic noise coming through the open windows, we had switched on a light and pulled out the guidebooks to search for another place to stay. Suddenly Donna began to read aloud, "If you are a hot and weary traveler searching for a "slice of air-conditioned heaven. . . ." As soon as it was daylight we had called the *pensione* in the book and fled to grab the available room.

"A slice of heaven"; I don't know of a better description for *Centro di Catechesi, Via degli Orsini,* 34. Nowadays, Sofia even has a strange-looking air conditioning unit that sits on the floor and is reputed to produce cool air, though I'm guessing she rarely uses it. In our conversations over the next three days, my chosen description is confirmed by an anecdote she shares about a priest who had visited the atrium in its beginning years and said: "This is truly heaven!"

I have proposed to Sofia a simple interview structure of three main topics for the three days: some highlights of the history, some revelations on the child and the work, and some of her hopes and concerns for the future.

I am comforted by the theological soundness of the number three, as well as by the agreement Sofia and I made long ago that whenever necessary I could lapse back into English and she could continue in Italian.

We seat ourselves by the windows nearest her desk where there are window boxes of geraniums and a view of her beloved clock tower in *Piazza Orologio*. I know and am grateful for the fact that she has chosen this spot for the interview because it affords us the most generous portion of light (the impossible-to-describe, golden Roman sunlight).

Sofia begins with a story. Many years ago, when she was in the United States to give a course, she found herself at New York's LaGuardia Airport needing to get to Kennedy airport in a very short time. Someone suggested that she might take a helicopter. "A helicopter?" She remembers the initial shock of the suggestion and then laughs over her response, "Why not!" She is excited to be remembering the thrill of that helicopter ride and recalls her feeling at that time that such an adventure was truly a "once-in-a-life-time" experience. As she was traveling back to her reality of studying, writing, and teaching in her chosen field of Jewish scholarship and her work with children in the atrium, she put the whole American experience in the same mental file as the helicopter ride: "exciting but finished."

Yet, the adventure has never ended. She marvels once again over how far and wide the Catechesis has spread and in such a variety of settings: "We never planned or imagined such growth. And what is most beautiful to realize is that this growth is not of our own making." Her delight seems fullest when she speaks of particular "shoots" of the work that have sprung up in mission sites such as the mountains of Bolivia, or in Mexico or Panama. I glance up to the bookshelf by her centuries-old, family heirloom desk where, for many years, she has displayed an obviously treasured photograph of some parents and their children making mud bricks to build their own atrium in a crowded, poor district of Mexico City.

When I ask how the adventure all began, almost the first word that comes out of her mouth is "Gianna," her closest and most beloved collaborator for almost all of these 50 years, until her death just six months prior to this interview. She speaks of Gianna's devotion to her family and her work with children in Montessori education, which began when she was a teenager and was assisting in Adele Costa Gnocchi's school. It was a school that accepted all children, including those with special needs. It had no formal name and, because of this fact, it was one of the few schools that were allowed to stay open during the fascist rule.

It was Costa Gnocchi who first recognized Gianna's rare gifts for working with children and encouraged her to pursue Montessori studies and practice rather than a career in academia. It was also Costa Gnocchi—the "matchmaker" (as I've come to think of her)—who introduced Sofia to "the child" as well as to Gianna. Sofia knew Costa Gnocchi through her aunts and began visiting her school while still in high school. She remembers how Costa Gnocchi would share just a word or two of wisdom on the child while Sofia was observing. Several years later, when Sofia had finished her university studies and was working with Eugenio Zolli as a Hebrew scholar, Costa Gnocchi would again be instrumental in drawing Sofia to a work with children.

I asked Sofia to say more about her relationship with Zolli, to whom she has always referred as "my master." She tells about how a friend at her university (La Sapienza) had first told her about this "amazing teacher" and had encouraged her to take a class in Hebrew with him. Sofia recalls her initial recoiling from the idea of studying yet another language, having just done intensive studies in Greek. Yet, from her first class with Zolli, she was hooked. She elaborates for a moment on the beautiful and engaging way he taught students the Hebrew alphabet and how he then took them directly to the translation of chapter 5 in Isaiah. She says that Zolli was already aware of the wisdom of the child when he accepted her invitation to come give a presentation to a group of children she was preparing for First Communion. She takes particular delight in telling how the children were so drawn to him, how they kept coming closer and closer to him "until they were practically in his arms."

In 1954 Costa Gnocchi had finally managed to persuade Sofia to give some Bible lessons to the grandson of a friend of Costa Gnocchi and two of his peers. The impact of her first direct experience of the child's relationship with God always reminds me of C. S. Lewis' book, *Surprised by Joy,* from which Sofia has quoted before. The atrium began from this very seed of joyful surprise. One of the things I most value in what Sofia has taught me is that, if you want to know the essence or true nature of a thing, you must look carefully at its origins.

It was in that same year, 1954, that Sofia met Gianna at Costa Gnocchi's school and they formally began the atrium in Sofia's home on Via degli Orsini. They began with only a few children, mostly six- and seven-year-olds, and only gradually began to include younger and younger children. In the Church at that time, children were not thought to be ready for the sacraments or for any formal religious education until the age of nine or ten. Although there was a movement afloat to consider younger children, there was no depth or real substance to the contents being offered them except, of course, in the case of Montessori's Barcelona experiment, which had come much earlier.

Sofia acknowledges how slow she and Gianna were to understand what they were observing in the children in those early years and how many errors they made. She refers to some of the early materials they made, which, along with some more recent materials, are now archived in the "materials reject closet" as an example of our tendency as adults to complicate and embellish things. But I am thinking that the "materials reject closet" is also a testimony to Sofia's and Gianna's profound humility before this mystery of God and the child to which they have dedicated their lives.

Sofia goes on to express her gratitude for the gift of having been able to work in her own environment for most of these 50 years. Only briefly did she ever work in a parish setting, yet she is both aware and respectful of the particular challenges, along with the particular joys, of parish ministry, which is the experience of most catechists. It was at a diocesan institute that Sofia gave her first catechist formation course, which she remembers as "a disaster." How happy she was to later move her adult courses to Via degli Orsini, where they have continued right up to today and are now being led by an *"ex-bambina"* of Sofia's atrium, Francesca Cocchini, and by Sandra Pollastri, a graduate of Sofia's adult courses.

Father Antonio Temofonte was the first priest who assisted them with atrium Masses. He was the provincial of an Italian order who had visited the atrium in its beginning years and apparently liked what he saw, referring to the atrium as "heaven," even though others at that time were critical of its seeming lack of moral education. (Who among us catechists of the Good Shepherd couldn't write a book on that subject!) It was Father Temofonte who accompanied Sofia to register the atrium with the diocese of Rome.

Sofia speaks of another relationship that led to the first international courses. She expresses her gratitude to A. M. Joosten for his significant role in the transplanting of her work to the United States and Mexico. Joosten, born in the Netherlands, was a leader in the Montessori movement who had given courses in India and the United States. He had also worked closely with Montessori in the Netherlands where he often accompanied her to Mass. After converting to Catholicism, Joosten visited Sofia's atrium and became the "insistent friend" who eventually persuaded her to come to

St. Paul, Minnesota, in 1975 to give a five-week course. Sofia is still amazed and touched by the fact that "Americans were even willing to give up their weekends." Two participants of that course carried the good news of the Catechesis home to Mexico, and within another year, Sofia had brushed up on her Spanish and headed there to give a course.

I remember when I had first come to study with Sofia and was feeling overwhelmed by the richness of the work and the atrium environment (all those materials I would need to make!). Sofia's words of comfort at that time were, "Not to worry; it is a long work." Among the many things that phrase has come to mean to me, I hear in it, "Be at peace; there is plenty of time. What is unfolding takes time, but it is worth all the effort, and it will last for a very long time" (forever, I think!). Among the greatest riches of the work of the Catechesis are the deep and lasting relationships that are formed. Sofia has opened every international gathering by acknowledging and cele-brating this gift that has come to us through our work with the children, because they involve us in what is most essential and brings the most joy.

Most who come to the Catechesis of the Good Shepherd and are for-tunate enough to live a common religious experience with children in the atrium remain (see Point #3 of the "Characteristics of the Catechesis of the Good Shepherd"). Tilde Cocchini came to Via degli Orsini to take a course with Sofia in the early years and ended up becoming the catechist of the six- to nine-year-olds, remaining until her death. Her education in the arts and her understanding of the child's artistic expression was a great gift to the work. Tilde's childlike wonder and enthusiasm, along with her devotion and generosity to the children of her atrium and the students of Sofia's courses (including myself), remain and continue to bless the atrium community.

Father Temofonte remained a friend of the atrium until his death, returning to celebrate a first Communion with the children, even after he moved from Rome. Father Giancarlo Pani, a Jesuit priest and friend of Francesca Cocchini at La Sapienza University, showed up at the atrium one day. He fell in love with the children and the children with him, and he has remained as their atrium priest for over 30 years.

Father Dalmazio Mongillo, a Dominican priest and former head of moral studies at the *Angelicum,* met Sofia at the home of mutual friends over 40 years ago. Some comment he made at the end of the evening let Sofia know immediately that he was a kindred spirit. He began frequent-ing her courses and she, his; a friendship and collaboration began that has never ended. Sofia points out that it was Mongillo who first recognized and

articulated the Catechesis of the Good Shepherd as celebration, the celebration of a relationship with God that is being nourished and given freedom of expression in the community of the atrium.

In these three days of conversations, Sofia speaks with affection and
gratitude about many others—adults and children—who have helped the
work to grow as well as added to her own joy. Later, when I'm home trying
to transcribe the tapes of our interview, I realize that her remembrances of
these collaborators permeate each of the three tapes and could fill an entire
book! One of my biggest challenges, therefore, has been that of having to
choose only a few of these anecdotes for this essay, so that there will be
space for sharing her answers to some "burning questions" I have for her:

*What about children of today; do you see them as different from the children
you began working with?* "No," she replies, "the deepest hungers remain
the same. What is different is the time it takes for children to reach silence.
The children who come to our atrium today are more distracted. It takes
longer for them to settle and focus, but once they do, their hunger and
capacity to respond to the kerygma is the same." Sofia sees that their "most
precious treasure—their capacity for joy—has somehow been preserved,
especially in the younger children, but also in the older ones. They can still
become so enchanted. We must not assume that they won't be able to do
this or that; we must try and see."

*What concerns you most not only about the work for the present but also for
the future?* "The tendency in the work to become too programmed, too
structured, too organized. This is the tendency we were addressing when
we began to speak long ago about the 'de-schooling of catechesis.' The children call us to a different way, a way of contemplation and enjoyment of
God, and this has been articulated in our 'characteristics' in describing the
atrium as a place of prayer. For children of today, who go so much and do
so much, the quiet and order and unhurried pace of the atrium becomes all
the more important. We must not overfeed; rather, we need to keep in mind
the marvelous capacities of the absorbent mind and all the child is receiving
in the atrium that has little or nothing to do with what we say or do as catechists. Truly, very little is needed. I remember a year in the 9 to 12 atrium
when we focused only on Abraham for the entire year, except, of course, for
those monthly atrium sessions when we prepared and celebrated the Mass.
To know one thing really well makes up for fifty other things that could
be known."

What about your hopes? What gives you the most hope for the future of the work? As I pose the question, I'm thinking of what she hopes will be done or accomplished, but her first answer is, "The child, the child's capacity for joy." Already in our conversations she has expressed her deep interest in learning more about the nature of the relationship that the child before three years of age has with God. Now she reiterates, "I hope very much that the Catechesis will go younger and younger." She also speaks of her interest and delight in the ecumenical experiences we've had at the adult level of our work, particularly the international retreat in Assisi several years ago that focused on Eucharist. "The child is naturally ecumenical. I hope that the tendency to emphasize our faith differences to children will end."

Finally I ask, *Can you say something about how the Catechesis has changed your life?* "It's the children who've changed my life. They have saved me from being a mouse in the library. I love to study; I always have, and I always will. But the children have made me more; they've given me the experience of life beyond the library; they've brought me into a life that includes helicopter rides!"

On my plane ride home and for these many months since the interview, as I've listened and re-listened to the tapes and have wrestled with how to do justice to Sofia's generous sharing of herself and the work, there is a particular quote of hers that I have savored most and that seems a fit ending to this essay. My only hesitation in sharing it is a familiar insecurity of mine as to whether I heard and have translated it exactly as she said it, but it's too beautiful not to try: "When something takes you where you do not know and yet, all along the way, God continues to provide, it is an adventure. And there is nothing more beautiful." In my head I hear the Rome atrium children singing the Abraham song I loved so much the first year I studied here: *"Esci dalla tua terra e va, dove ti mostrero."* (Leave your homeland and go to a land I will show you.) Thanks be to God for Sofia and Gianna and for the wonderful adventure of the Catechesis.

Catechesis as Celebration

Dalmazio Mongillo, OP

I would like to reflect on the work of Sofia Cavalletti and Gianna Gobbi, who have shared a long experience of catechesis with children since 1954. But first I would like to clarify my perspective on catechesis, thinking in particular of children from three to six years of age. Catechesis, in my view, is to learn to live in the family of God, to grow together in the sharing of the same life and in the vital recognition of the love in which each of us is loved.

Catechesis is to let ourselves be loved and saved. It is to nurture the desire of the Shepherd, to remain in his love, to rediscover the conditions and the essential needs of life lived in communion, and to support each other in seeking the way to actualize it. Catechesis grows in continuity with the experience described in the first letter of John (1 John 1:1–5).

I would identify catechesis as concelebration. It is the concelebration of a gathering of the people of God, in Jesus Christ, who acknowledge the Father, in which each person, along with all the others, discovers oneself to be loved and included in a journey of life. This journey of life leads each one of us to become the subject of God's initiative, empowered to receive and to give, aware of our personal responsibilities, and conscious of ourselves as persons who are known, called, and accepted by God, as king, prophet, and priest (1 Peter 2:5ff). It is a life journey in which we become persons who listen, speak, and contribute to the building up of the family of God in an osmosis of life with the Father.

The celebration of catechesis is growth in the faith operating in charity (Galatians 5:6). We participate in this celebration when we receive and live it, in the listening and belonging that grafts us into the life-giving communication circuit of agape.

In this perspective, the experience of Sofia Cavalletti and Gianna Gobbi confirms, without any possibility of equivocation, that simultaneity of giving and receiving, of listening and proclaiming, which is lived in the community that is joined together in the Shepherd. The most surprising dimension of their experience relates to young children who, when they feel themselves to be accepted by persons who are living in agape, really do open themselves and grow in freedom, allowing themselves to become involved, to let go of resistances and defenses, and spontaneously support the action of the teacher within them. It is the child's original state that needs to be cultivated, and in which the child needs to be grounded so as to be received as a child of the kingdom (Matthew 18:3).

Catechesis becomes much more authentic the more that those who live and participate in it, each according to one's own condition, experience the joy of recognizing themselves as united in the same life, going forward on the journey of the loving knowledge of the same truth. On this journey each person, with one's unique task, praises the Father, listens to and contemplates the mystery of God, manifests and shares what has been experienced, and accepts the call to transform life in the service of the full dignity of all persons. In the perspective of catechesis as concelebration, the most loved concelebrant is certainly the child. Contrary to what is generally thought, the child is endowed with unsuspected capacities for koinonia, for communion; the child has a specific receptivity, a simple, clear conaturality with the love of God in Jesus Christ.

The catechist needs to recognize the draw of the Father, which attracts the child (John 6:44), nourishing these seeds in the child and, in delicately attending to this, the catechist grows in the fullness of redeemed personhood. The recognition of the Father in Jesus will be more alive to the degree that the communion in which this little family lives is alive, in its respect for each person's path, and in its acceptance, awareness, and building up of the church. This family lives as joined together in the Lord's name (Matthew 18:20) and opens itself in caring for the whole of reality of which it is a part. In the family of God, we grow as persons when we do not pose resistance to the working of the Father; we learn to know and discern God's voice, to support God's work for the good of all, to respect the stages of growth of each person, and to safeguard the rights of each person.

The Christian proclamation does not take place simply with the spoken announcement of truths, but where the proclamation is lived by persons who are united in the same communion of life (1 John 1:1–5). The validity of the experience of Sofia Cavalletti and Gianna Gobbi seems to me to be rooted precisely in this vital osmosis that unites and transforms the small community where the proclamation is offered, received, lived, and communicated. Their experience makes evident how the Christian message satisfies the child's deep need for spontaneity, naturalness, and sharing, when it is proclaimed in conditions that correspond to the structure of the child.

It is not about a new methodology, as a substitute for others; its "new-ness" resides in the inspiration from which it originates, and in light of this inspiration all the forms into which it has been translated and expressed should be read. If someone tries to ascribe its effectiveness to having hit upon just the "right" parable, we need to recall the truth so often reiterated by Augustine and Thomas Aquinas: Even the letter of the Gospel would die were it not for the Spirit speaking within the heart. If someone maintains that it is centered in that space reserved for the "creativity" of the child, it should be pointed out that the finest fruit of this "journey" is not a more intense inventiveness, but rather the peace and deep joy in the encounter with Jesus, the child's openness to listening, the delicacy of the relationship that is being established in the child with the Father, and the capacity to love.

I neither undervalue nor minimize the methodological elements of this catechesis. However, I am convinced that the source of everything is in searching together in deep harmony and in the atmosphere of mystery, which blossoms in the koinonia between the children living in the Father's attraction and the person who recognizes and supports it, because the cate-chist is also drawn into that communion. The church is built up and grows in the acceptance of the drawing power of the Father, who invites the docile, spontaneous receptivity of the child and the discreet, delicate interaction of the catechist.

So as not to misrepresent God's great masterpiece or cause another misinterpretation, it is necessary to highlight clearly that catechesis with children is the "joyful contemplation" of the action of the Holy Spirit in the hearts of the children whom the Spirit loves; as such, it is the respectful attentiveness to the ways that nourish their growth, so that the dialogue between the Spirit and the bride not be disturbed.

It is not merely a matter of standing there watching this action of the Spirit, but rather of taking part in it, of sharing in it: the announcement, the listening, the prayer, the invitation to personalize it are all without substi-tute. Our respectful attentiveness is what moves us to step aside at the opportune moment, so that we leave space for the child's dialogue with the inner teacher, and not divert its growth.

Nor is catechesis simply a matter of accustoming children to learn-ing certain gestures or saying certain words. Instead it is guiding children toward a tactile, living experience of the relationship with the Shepherd, with themselves, with the other sheep and the sheepfold; it is to support children when they become conscious of the existence of the lost sheep and hired hand, and thus, of conflict and weakness.

To "touch" the Shepherd, sheep, sheepfold is the experience of the "sacramentality of the faith." It comes to birth and grows when the person, in the community of faith, enters into relationship with the Shepherd who saves, experiencing the delicacy of his hand that touches and caresses, accepting his invitation to transmit the gift of love. Even in faith the person knows the reality one is touching, with which one is familiar.

With the Shepherd who feeds us in the Eucharist, who speaks to us in the scriptures, and who sustains us along the path of justice and communion, our fears are diminished, our responsibilities become clearer, and we realize the truth as total light. And the Shepherd is not an object of study or research; he is love to love, nourishment to eat, blood to receive into the circulation of our very existence, beauty to contemplate, word to be listened to, life to be shared, body to give us growth (1 John 1:1–5). In the signs through which the Shepherd enters into contact with us, he transforms us, he makes us become Church, sacrament capable of cultivating and fostering the mysterious koinonia, which makes of the human creature a child in the home of the Father. Faith is life, and life generates, and this life is transmitted in the family that lives in faith.

The proclamation makes us become listeners; it gives us eyes to see and ears to hear. The proclamation is born and grows in Jesus Christ, "pioneer and perfecter of our faith" (Hebrews 12:2) who, through the community of the apostles ("Indeed, in Christ Jesus I became your father through the gospel" [1 Corinthians 4:15]), lives in the families joined together in his name, in the little gatherings of his Church.

The proclamation that feeds faith is not the act of speaking; it is the continuity of the creative action of the Lord, who desired the existence of all that is, pronounced their names, called them forth and they came into being and lived (Genesis 1:1–31). The proclamation is the fruit of love, which generates life when it is given as a gift, when it is spoken, offered with the words and gestures that are its instruments, that overflow from a heart which gives itself in the initiative of letting oneself become involved.

An indefinite range of excuses distracts us from going forward along this journey; they imprison us in the shifting sands of intellectualism that slow us in entrusting ourselves to love. To help ourselves to unveil and release these excuses is a responsibility we all share. The experience of Sofia Cavalletti and Gianna Gobbi, nurtured in their deep inspiration and embodied in the forms in which it is actively expressed, will help to make great strides toward the maturation of a style of catechesis that advances "the way of God."

Translated by Patricia Coulter

With Prayer We Speak to God

Silvana Quattrocchi Montanaro, MD

The Catechesis of the Good Shepherd is 50 years old, exactly the age of my first daughter, Giulia. The opportunity to know this catechesis came to me through Giulia.

But let us proceed with order. While I was expecting my first child, a lady who worked in my husband's office asked permission for her sister to observe my newborn during the first days immediately after birth. When I met this woman's sister, she introduced herself as a student in a course she was taking to become a Montessori Assistant to Infancy. She explained that the course was directed by Adele Costa Gnocchi, a former professor of philosophy and pedagogy at a women's college in Rome. Adele had been a participant in the first course for directresses of the *Casa dei Bambini* given by Maria Montessori in 1909. Since then, Adele had become a great admirer and friend of Montessori. Adele started a Montessori school in Rome that survived when all other Montessori schools closed during the fascist era. When Montessori returned to Italy, after her long exile in India, she urged Adele to create a course that would prepare special people to become Assistants to Infancy. In the new course, students would learn how to interact with infants and how to prepare a suitable environment to facilitate "education from birth." Montessori felt that "at three a child is too old and the most important time of human development has already passed."

When my baby was born, this student came to the Maternity Hospital and for many hours every day she observed the child and wrote her observations. She gave me information about her studies and told me that the director of the course had opened a *scuoletta* (little school) for children from 18 months on in a building called *Palazzo Taverna.*

When my daughter reached that age, I remembered what the student had said about the little school. I went there with my child and rang at the door. Meeting Adele Costa Gnocchi has been for me a memorable event, and my personal and professional life were completely changed by this encounter. Adele told me that in Via degli Orsini 34, there was a special place for religious education. So I met Sofia!

Giulia, and later Marina (my second daughter), went to the atrium. One day, when I arrived to pick up my daughters, Giulia (at that time four-and-a-half) showed me a piece of paper on which she had written with uncertain calligraphy: *"nella preghiera parliamo a Dio"* (with prayer we speak to God). Even now I cannot completely explain why that affirmation produced such a strong and profound emotion in me, but I certainly had a very powerful experience of an "essential reality of Christian life through the child." All catechists know how special the children's prayers in our atria are, especially the prayers of the very young ones. As a mother, I felt a responsibility to understand more deeply the work done in the atrium so that I could better help my children in their spiritual journey. I discovered that a course for catechists was being offered in Via degli Orsini and imme-diately decided to do it. At this point I had three children and a fourth one on the way!

The first day I brought my third child Valerio to Adele Costa Gnocchi's *scuoletta,* I met, in the entrance, a mother with her child; this mother was Tilde Cocchini with her son Andrea. From that moment a rela-tionship started between us that became in time a very deep friendship; we were linked together through the Montessori work in our schools and the Catechesis of the Good Shepherd course that we took together. During the course, Sofia lectured, and any time she needed to quote from the Bible, she read from the original texts (in Greek and Hebrew), and many times (almost always) she was profoundly unsatisfied with the translation we had in our hands. Sofia expended a lot of effort trying to give the students the right meaning of the original words, and this situation made me seriously consider the idea of learning Hebrew. At that point all of my four children were going to Montessori schools, and my mornings were relatively free, so I became a student of the Biblical Institute for five years.

When Adele Costa Gnocchi discovered my medical training, she asked me to lecture about obstetrics, nutrition, and hygiene in the Assistants to Infancy course. Adele was an extraordinary person, and many times, after my lectures to the students, she would talk to me about the situation of very young children, how their potential was not understood and how Montessori's discovery was still not recognized in the world. Her remarks helped me to study better the Montessori books that focus especially on the importance of the first years of life when the human being is "a psychic embryo." I also took the Assistants to Infancy course and met Mario and Ada Montessori when they came to visit their friend Adele at the school in Rome. So in addition to my pediatrics profession, I entered the Montessori world.

In 1979 Mario invited me to participate in the congress in Amsterdam to mark the 50-year anniversary of the Association Montessori International; there I gave a presentation on the Montessori approach for prenatal life, birth, and the first years. After that speech some people from the audience proposed that I give a two-week seminar in Tarrytown, New York, that coming July. The same summer Sofia was supposed to give a course in Mexico City, but she became sick and asked me to do it when my workshop in the United States was completed. I accepted with enthusiasm, and thus began my teaching in our catechesis. Since then, I have gone back to Mexico with Sofia and Gianna many times, and we have also traveled together in Israel.

Later, and for many years, I took responsibility in the atrium for the group of adolescents preparing for confirmation. In the hours we spent together in prayer and meditation on the Bible, I have been greatly enriched in my spiritual life, especially in trying to understand the Person and the work of the Holy Spirit, promised by Jesus to all of us upon his return to the Father. The greatest discovery has been that we have this special gift from the resurrected Christ inside us, and that we can do more than he himself did when he lived on earth (John 14:12): we can multiply food, heal the sick, resuscitate the dead! We are all amazed.

Psychology teaches us that we can only do what we feel capable of, so our self-image plays an important role in our actions. Our degree of self-esteem is very important for how we engage in life. This preparation for confirmation helps us to experience a profound consolation: we have the active force of God inside us, and with this help everything is possible! This fact is important for everyone, but especially for persons in the delicate developmental period of adolescence, the time when children often feel insecure in front of the new role they must assume in life. To reach an awareness of the incredible inner strength that comes from the Holy Spirit, that faithful companion who lives in us, can be the greatest help in finding the courage to use all our energies to perform our personal work in God's cosmic plan. A lot of discouragement, pessimism, and dissatisfaction come from not fully using this great potential, our talents, that we have received from our Father since birth. All through the third plane of development, human beings long to achieve something important, but too often we cannot find the impetus to commit ourselves totally in life because we lack self-confidence. We lack self-confidence because, in our early years, we are not given proper help to experience success in our work. The family, the school, and the Church should collaborate to provide young children the means to achieve this success so that later we would be able to become aware of how much we can accomplish when we count on the special support of God's Spirit. What a great responsibility for parents, educators, and all adults! Montessori called adolescence "a new birth," and these special newborns, with their searching and their insights, have helped me to discover a better role for adults when dealing with them.

The 50-year anniversary of Sofia's and Gianna's first atrium is for me a cherished opportunity to look back at the last 50 years of my life and to acknowledge how important Sofia's and Gianna's work has been to me. I wish, in union with all the people working in this catechesis, to give thanks for the great gift of having discovered, with the children and because of the children, that we are loved, called by name, and asked to enter into the perennial covenant with God. With the children and because of the children, we have developed the capacity of wonder in front of the Good Shepherd's love, and we have received the reassuring certainty that nothing can separate us from him.

Let me also express my deep feelings of gratitude to the Good Shepherd who, through my relationships with children, adolescents, and catechists, helped me so much and in such a special way, in my personal journey toward him.

Let us continue to be united around the children, and let us continue to pray with them until: "There will be one flock, one shepherd" (John 10:16) and "God may be all in all" (1 Corinthians 15:28). Amen!

An Opening into the Way of Love

Luigi Capogrossi

When I recall my experience working with Sofia Cavalletti, in my mind her image is always linked with the memory of Adele Costa Gnocchi, the great and unforgettable friend of Maria Montessori, whose "little school" I attended in my childhood years (beginning from 1939 or 1940). My parents and I enjoyed a great friendship with Costa Gnocchi up until her death. In the early 1960s, Costa Gnocchi introduced me to a new experience, the method of religious formation for children inaugurated by Sofia in Via degli Orsini.

Miss Costa Gnocchi had a winning way about her; she was able to draw all kinds of people and experiences into the net of her interests, developed through her vocation as an educator. Thus she aroused my interest by making a number of quick, repeated references to a new experience with children, a method of religious education that did not impose a curriculum from outside, but instead simply facilitated the child's religious potential and gave direction in a manner appropriate to each child's developmental stage. Costa Gnocchi explained to me that this experience had been initiated and developed by Sofia together with her close collaborator, Gianna Gobbi. Though I happened to know Gianna from way back, for she had been one of my teachers at the "little school" in Palazzo Taverna, I did not yet know Sofia.

The idea that one might foster the child's natural inclination to live in relationship to God, rather than creating a mold in which to force the child's soul, was the bait that Adele Costa Gnocchi, in her wisdom and with subtle patience, used to hook me. She persuaded me to join in launching a new association, the Maria Montessori Association for the Religious Formation of the Child. In Costa Gnocchi's mind, I was destined to be its president.

And so, in 1962, with Rosa Russo Jervolino, Adelaide Balmas, Mrs. Durio, Mrs. Nobilioni, and others, I went to a notary's office to form the new association. The initial goal of this association was to support and strengthen the organizational efforts, the burden of which, until that time, had rested completely on Sofia's and Gianna's shoulders. The association's chief role was to provide organizational support, and so it has remained over the years, even as the association has experienced an extraordinary growth far outside Rome and the few Italian towns where this method first began. Obviously, though, the common work with Sofia and Gianna and the various recurrent problems for which they sought my help in solving brought me closer to many aspects of their formative work with the children; therefore, my initial visit to the notary's office also marked the beginning of a long, uninterrupted relationship with Sofia and Gianna, as well as the start of a new spiritual adventure for me as an adult, because the Catechesis of the Good Shepherd had not been a reality for me in my childhood.

My role as president of the association, though well defined, was vague. Beyond my formal duties (a president for life, in violation of every legal statute but at the behest of Sofia and Gianna), I helped to cope with practical matters that, especially at first, were troublesome. Among the early concerns, there was a continual lack of funds needed for the work, a dearth of people in Italy willing to commit themselves to this experience and, above all, the halting progress of this project, which eventually involved greater numbers of centers and children. I felt more and more like the benign counselor of a group that was active, competent, strongly motivated, and in close contact with Gianna and Sofia.

Gianna's deep sense of security in her perception of the child and the nature of the relationship to be built with him was in contrast to how easily she could be disturbed by every problem to do with legal or institutional issues that could not be cleared up at once. Sofia, too, had many concerns involving organizational and institutional problems, which became entangled by ever more complex interpersonal relations, as her work gradually made an impact in different parts of the world. All of a sudden, usually in the morning, I would receive a phone call from Sofia who, in a gentle voice and somewhat anxiously, would consult me for advice on how to go about things, on how best to resolve issues, settle disputes, and make rules of conduct. And then there were the little meetings in Sofia's living room, not only with her and Gianna but also with Tilde and Claudio Cocchini, and later with their daughter Francesca, Adelaide Balmas, and Silvana Montanaro. In all these conversations, my purpose was to calm Gianna's and Sofia's anxieties. Yet I felt like a placebo because the mental relief I gave was a mere reflection of the great competence of my partners in dialogue. I only repeated back to them the deep-rooted truth, which resided in these unwitting bearers of light.

From our little meetings and frequent communications, I grew to know these two persons, Sofia and Gianna, who were so closely allied and yet so different.

In Gianna I relived my own peasant roots; she was similarly rooted in the landscape of central Italy, so important not just for her but also for Adele Costa Gnocchi and the origins of the Montessori movement. And I was deeply amused by her suspicion of every imaginable legal trap and by her need for clear definitions, which reflected a vivid, peasant's respect for things and for people. Gianna spoke so articulately because she was a woman who needed clarity, the clarity of the countryside of the Marches, where the shape of things is clear-cut, full of sunshine, and without nuances. Her anxiety over vagueness, over every hint of ambiguity, gave me cause to smile affectionately because, as a lawyer, I know full well that nothing is more uncertain than the certainty of the law.

Sofia is different. In her I have perceived a latent tension between a marked social manner and sobriety of style, on the one hand, and an adventurous spirit, on the other. As reticent and shy as Gianna was when it came to exploring foreign territory, Sofia has always been open and ready for adventure. No new organizational experiment, field of action, or opportunity for new encounters can seem too big or too dangerous to Sofia. Not that she has ever displayed any form of imprudence, superficiality, or impulsiveness. On the contrary, from the way her many books are strewn about the small living room where she works, you can see that she is a true professional, a hardworking scholar, a real authority on the different aspects of the religious tradition her actions are rooted in, and a bookworm of the academic sort. Furthermore, she does not need to advertise her deep piety (which is shared by all the others who have taken part in the adventure), for it is the very essence of her life. And Sofia is never self-righteous; indeed, when any hint of self-righteousness or hidebound rigidity has ever emerged from a temporary participant in our association, Sofia's detached attitude would be unmistakable to those who have known her, even if concealed from the offender behind Sofia's good manners. Sofia's aristocratic bearing and expressions do not obscure the extraordinary freedom of a spirit that embodies the Gospel, saying, "Truth will set you free." This freedom often expresses itself in a subtle but perceptible impatience with mediocrity and shallowness. Perhaps, more than anything else, my admiration for these traits has drawn me near to Sofia over the years, resulting in a close friendship, seldom cloaked in words but made of an intangible and rare substance, a combination of respect and mutual understanding.

Despite all their important qualities, the most striking thing about Sofia and Gianna was (and continues to be with Sofia) their openheartedness to children, an attitude I had already observed in Costa Gnocchi. Gianna and Sofia have been more like interpreters and guides than like teachers. And so, the experience of the Catechesis of the Good Shepherd came into being, not so much as a result of a project imposed from on high and fine-tuned in a sterile environment, but as the natural expression of its leading figures, the children.

The Early Years

In the early years of the association, the two main fields of work we focused on were the spread of this experience, through supporting and coordinating the work of individual centers, and material support, scant though our capabilities were due to the voluntary nature of our association. In all matters, however, the association merely followed Sofia's and Gianna's lead and gave whatever counsel the two women might request in order to help solve any problem that arose in their many undertakings.

Even while the work of training the trainers and the "courses" given at Via degli Orsini was in the capable hands of these two major forces and their closest collaborators, their relations with the religious authorities were sometimes shaky. In the Diocese of Rome, Sofia's personal relations with the Church authorities and their high opinion of her were able to pare down, but not do away with, every problem. The spiritual dimension of Sofia's approach and the formative nature of her project were too different from the firmly established rules in traditional religious education. The quite understandable Roman sense of caution made it difficult to find a real response within the structures of the Church. Not without reason, the parishes in Rome, and in Italy in general, were more reluctant to enter new relationships and more resistant to the introduction of a new type of religious education than parishes in other nations that were younger and more open to new ideas.

In time, though, the growing success of the Catechesis of the Good Shepherd in far-off lands became evident. The annual reports of the association, which Sofia faithfully prepared, recorded the extraordinary growth of her undertaking and its spreading influence; new centers arose throughout the world, from Canada to the United States, from Mexico to Colombia, in African and European countries. The Good Shepherd method spread in a most impressive manner, and the local bishops slowly became interested. The story of this success belongs to all those who now take part in this experience. It is not for me to flesh it out.

This growth called me to reflect anew on the problems of coordination and the challenge to unite faithfully the many different people and the diverse centers with the method and contents of the Good Shepherd system of religious education. From the way these aspects have formed a harmonious unit, I have come to appreciate, over these past years, Sofia's and Gianna's extraordinary capacity for direction and inspiration. And this unity is all the more vital and productive as a result of the marked differences in Sofia's and Gianna's characters, which I noted before. Their divergent opinions would give rise to discussions involving us all, discussions that always resulted in a positive and practical solution, cemented by friendship.

Friendship is an important element in the growth and vitality of this method, no less important than religious zeal and attention to what the child already is and is gradually becoming by natural inclination. Friendship is the key to the story of Gianna and Sofia, to the story of the growth of the Catechesis of the Good Shepherd, and to the story of the association. This spirit of friendship has spread worldwide and has embraced, time and again, the unflaggingly enthusiastic participants in this experience. They have transplanted this method and helped it grow in many different countries and in many different languages.

My recollection of every meeting, nationally and then internationally, is associated with this sense of community, built on a common project and bonded by friendship. And at the center, always, to provide balance and stability are Sofia and Gianna.

This emphasis on friendship has helped us to overcome obvious personal differences and problems that arise when people with dissimilar characters and interpretations come together to work on a common project. Sofia and Gianna have continually used the language of friendship, both to guide the work of each community and to enrich the life of each center, in a work made complex by the growing dimensions of this experience.

What really won me over was an episode concerning a child, which Adele Costa Gnocchi used to lure me into this adventure, over 40 years ago. A boy, whom Sofia and Gianna had prepared for First Communion, copied a Gospel passage onto a holy card as a keepsake of the event; he chose Luke 24:32, wherein the apostles realize that Jesus had been among them. My old friend Costa Gnocchi made it plain to me, and even today that boy's choice still strikes me as a splendid witness to the depth of religious understanding which motivated that little boy. He was able to perceive the divine presence as a loss that gives rise to an insatiable need. Hearing this episode was the only way my ravaged, though not dead, religious sense could awaken to a new spiritual adventure. As always, Adele Costa Gnocchi was able to find that way. I chose the same Gospel passage to be written on my mother's gravestone, because I, along with the boy and the apostles in this Gospel account, share this sense of something very big, something too big for us, which is grasped only when we have lost it.

I have worn many hats in my professional life and have played more or less major roles. But, as I look back, perhaps only my light duty as president of the association has been an unfailingly positive experience. Sofia and Gianna have always expressed their deep gratitude for the help they say I have given them and for everything that other friends of the association have done in cooperation with them. Now the time has come for me to express my gratitude, not just for their friendship, not only for their charm, sincerity, and for the good cheer I experienced during the many hours we spent together, but for something I have received from them, something hard to put into words; I am deeply grateful for my sense of an inner peace that has been present in each of them and for their way of doing things with a deep and undaunted serenity that I have imbibed and continually savored in the hours after our meetings. Finally, and above all, I am most grateful for a sense of something precious I have encountered, though without fully comprehending it.

In a world full of hate, amid epoch-making catastrophes, above all in the realm of emotional life, that humanity seems to bring upon itself, a world where a spirit of death and hate and intolerance increasingly hovers, a small group of people have worked, under Sofia's guidance and with Gianna's special contribution, so that every human being, together with life itself, may discover an opening into the way of love and that natural holiness which is hidden in everyone's heart. Gianna's and Sofia's work provides a witness to help us understand that this deep-seated spirit of love and respect are not an adjunct to life, but the condition for its very existence.

And so, looking back on my memories of Tilde and Gianna, who have passed away, I can say once again: "Did not our hearts burn within us when he talked to us on the road?"

Translated by Father Joseph Occhio, SDB

Memories of Forty Years in the Atrium

Patrizia Cocchini

I am a catechist at the Center of Catechesis of the Good Shepherd in Rome; however, before becoming a catechist, I was a child in the atrium of Sofia Cavalletti and Gianna Gobbi. My sister Francesca and I had Professor Cavalletti as our religion teacher during our high school years, and it was she who called upon Professor Tommaso Federici, a liturgist and an expert in Judaism at the Pontifical University Urbaniana, to prepare us for confirmation.

We were a group of ten children, and the lessons were quite serious and labor intensive. We would read directly from the Bible, comment on it, and penetrate the rituals of the sacraments. We began to learn words such as *kerygma, typology,* and *parousia.* Professor Federici urged us to study always with a critical and selective spirit and to check everything—assertions, readings from original texts, citations. Meanwhile, Sofia would hold special lessons for us on the Torah. We would sit in her study, as one would in a *yeshiva* (Hebrew school), each with our own personal Bible on our laps, listening to the Word, and falling in love. Our eyes were opened to a new vision of religion linked to joy. We learned how to pray with the psalms. We felt ourselves inserted into the history of salvation, not by chance, but because we had been chosen and called by God.

After confirmation Sofia could have ended it all, but no, instead she came up with other things for us to study. They were always more difficult, but gradually became more understandable, such as lessons on theology and exegesis with Father Giovanni Rossetto, a professor of biblical studies. So it came to be that from age 14 to age 18 we continued our lessons through a set of classes Professor Rossetto gave university students earning their bachelor's degree in biblical studies.

We had it tough for a few years, understanding little and listening much. Yet the Word was doing its work within us, just like the grain of wheat in the dark and, apparently, indifferent earth. In this way we began to know about literary genres, to analyze Hebrew, Greek, and Latin scripture texts, to compare ancient versions with more modern ones, and to know about eschatology. Afterward, we would meet with Sofia in her studio and make comments on what we had learned together.

The strange thing was that we felt committed, in a mysterious way I would say, to go every Saturday afternoon to the atrium of the Good Shepherd. We gathered in the room that is currently the atrium of the youngest children but was then reserved for the adults, in order to listen to the Synoptic Gospels, the commentaries of various exegetes, and the points of view of other Christian confessions.

Even our school friends would respect our appointment with the Bible during those afternoons, which had previously always been dedicated to parties and movies; they would move our recreation time to another afternoon. They would do this without a word of reproach and without any show of displeasure, which still remains a mystery to me. Perhaps they could see the seriousness and the importance of these lessons for us.

When we finished this course Sofia did not lose sight of us. Rather, as I mentioned before, she could invent a thousand beautiful ways to entice us toward the Word of God. Hence, my sister and I started to take a course on Bible and liturgy for catechists, which Sofia gave for the vicariate of Rome.

These lessons were held twice a week. The lessons on the Bible were given by Sofia; the lessons on catechetical practices were given by Gianna; and the lessons on Montessori methodology were given by Flaminia Guidi and Maria Teresa Marchetti. Gianna was professor of Montessori technical applications at the high school level. From her we learned how important it is to go to the essential in all things, to make our movements more precise, to keep order within and about ourselves, to live without rushing, and to trust our own good sense.

Then there was the matter of final exams, which were quite difficult and fear-inspiring, for they were conducted in a very formal way in the offices of the vicariate of Rome. As we were preparing for them, we thought to ourselves that, if we should get questions from Sofia, we would do well to start the discussion with the word "Abraham," because it was such a well-loved name for her. If we should be asked questions by Gianna, then we would do well to begin with the words "Maria Montessori," who was for Gianna the only true educator. For Flaminia Guidi, the magic word was "child."

I was already enrolled in a medical degree program and would alternate those studies with catechetical studies, becoming so passionate about the latter that Sofia suggested that my mother, my sister Francesca, and I continue our studies with a course on Hebrew languages at the SIDIC (International Jewish-Christian Documentation Service) with Professor Arzieli. After completing this course, we went on to an intense course of biblical Hebrew with Rabbi Segre and Professor Piattelli.

In 1967, my mother, my sister, and I opened an atrium in a parish on the outskirts of Rome with children of various social classes. It was there that Pope John Paul II came to visit us in 1983 and where he remained awhile, struck by the silence and by the sight of the children working with the materials. My mother explained all of these things to the pope, conducting a real catechesis for him on that afternoon visit.

I remember with what great love and joy we designed and made all the materials. We worked on them an entire summer while on vacation in the mountains: the prayers of the Sacramentary, the history strip, the boxes for the dioramas, the poster boards for the typology work, the anthologies of the Bible, the drawings and the explanations of the sacraments; only the miniature vestments of the priest were sewn by someone else.

In 1971 and in 1973 we experienced two beautiful trips to Israel with Sofia and the Bible in order to reconstruct within us, step by step, all the history of our patriarchs, of our home, of our roots.

The trip to Israel was not just a visit to the places where Jesus had lived and spoken or where the history of Israel unfolded and continues to unfold but, thanks to Sofia, it was also a meeting with persons she knew, Jews and Christians, who communicated to us the love they felt toward that land.

Among these people, I remember a priest, Father Bruno Hussar, in a special way. He summarized within his own person not only the contradictions, but also the hope of that land. He was, as he used to say, truly a Christian and a priest, truly a Jew, truly an Israelite, and also one born in Egypt, an Arab country. He founded the house of St. Isaiah in Jerusalem, a Dominican center for Jewish studies where the Mass was celebrated in Hebrew, and also the *Nevé Shalom* ("village of peace," a name taken from Isaiah 32:18), a place where Jews and Arabs live together to this day.

I remember Michele Tagliacozzo, an Italian Jew living in Israel, who wished to pray with us and who called Mary the most beautiful daughter of Israel. Among the places that we visited, I particularly remember the cave of Qumran, where the discovery of Bible scrolls took place in the silence of the desert that completely surrounds it. Also, I remember the songs of the synagogue of Chassidim, which reached the requisite number of ten people when we entered, permitting us to pray together in a loud voice.

With us was Father Giancarlo Pani, who has helped us so much over the years in Sofia's atrium, following the children and becoming a point of reference for them, and when they have grown up, the children are able to find in him a priest-friend.

Those were the post–Vatican II days of the Church's openness toward the laity and toward women. The Mass was no longer in Latin, and the eucharistic table was placed in front of the people; all participated in the death and Resurrection of Christ with increasing awareness.

The group from Via degli Orsini—as we called ourselves, using the name of the street of Sofia's atrium—could not fail to participate in this important change. Had we not learned, since we were small children in the atrium, as a matter of fact, that the liturgy and the Bible are the center of Christian life and that all sacraments converge on the sacrament of the Eucharist?

That was how we began thinking about celebrating a Mass of "our own," put together by us: adults, young people, and children. We had the opportunity to use a chapel in the center of Rome, close to Piazza del Popolo. Every Sunday, one of us would take turns "guiding" a liturgy there. In order to avoid falling into intellectualism we would often repeat: "Make sure that the little old lady in the back of the church can understand you!" Federica Mastroianni, and Chicca and Luisa Gobbi would play the guitars and even the choice of songs was done in community. There was nothing in the Mass that we did not prepare.

In 1973, the priest who celebrated our Mass had us participate in a congress on Marxism and Christianity held by the Jesuit priest Father Diez-Alegria, a congress which made us aware that, despite the Church's culpability in not always making the choices of Christ during the course of its history, we could remain in the Church because we could assume an attitude of "conversion." In those years the temptation to a "secularized" faith was posed in order to contrast pre–Vatican II religiosity. But, according to Father Diez-Alegria, religiosity should be of an ethical-prophetic kind: The God of the prophets is the God who, based on love and based on justice among human beings, holds us accountable. There is no love without justice.

In those days our horizons were opened to the liberty affirmed by the Second Vatican Council, which helped us greatly in the adventure upon which we would shortly embark with Sofia. Sofia was, in fact, asking herself at that time what she could offer children who left the atrium after ten years. There was the Saturday afternoon Mass, but the Thursday afternoon reflection to prepare for it was more appropriate for adults than for preadolescent children. It was then that Sofia thought of arranging a catechetical course for confirmation which would be given by us young people, who were in our twenties: Claudio Conforti, Alberto Biagi, Francesco De Rosa, Pasquale and Nicoletta Lanciano, and my sister Francesca and I; and also involving another group of young people ages 16 to 17 who would help us by acting as a bridge to boys and girls around age 12. We would call the group of teens "catechist-assistants."

Including this last group of assistants was Sofia's way of not "leaving behind" even one of the atrium's "ex-children," who had already received confirmation but were not old enough or sufficiently prepared to guide a confirmation group by themselves. So we formed groups of ten children, ages 12 to 13 years old, who were guided by one of us as catechist and by a catechist-assistant.

The experience inspired enthusiasm. It happened like this: Wednesday afternoon, we, "the older ones," would meet and prepare the topics for meditation in Sofia's studio. Afterward, each of us would prepare for the meeting with the boys and girls with our catechist-assistant. The meetings would take place, by turns, in the home of a candidate for confirmation, to give a sense of hospitality. Naturally, Sofia had thought of beginning each meeting with a reading of the Word of God. The initiative is always God's. The first scripture passage, in the beginning of the confirmation course, was chosen by Sofia with care: Isaiah 11 (the shoot that comes from the stump of Jesse). In fact, who better than the adolescent can see in his or her own self those changes that noiselessly happen within one's own body, in one's own sensibility, in one's own world?

We poured out all we knew, all our *innamoramento* ("to fall in love") with God, on these girls and boys. We responded to all their questions, asked questions along with them, and searched for the answers together in the Bible. Of course, each one of us had our own personal Bible.

They were children who had experienced the Catechesis of the Good Shepherd from the time they had been 3 or 4 years old; yet . . . how much wonder . . . how much amazement was in them as we read with them about

God's choice of the smallest: the choice of David, close behind his flock; of Abraham the nomad; of Moses, slave of the Pharaoh! But the wonder was also in us, because the Word of God is always a parable: The more you read it, the more you discover treasures and pearls.

The second year, the themes were "liberation" and "the law as gift." We would meditate on the problem of pain and, because our faith is a nuptial celebration, we would read the Song of Songs. Our relationship with God is a relationship of love; He has chosen us and has called us only because He loves us. We would later go and research in the liturgy everything we had read in the Bible. We studied the rites of the sacraments, which we had given to the boys and girls at the beginning of the course in a solemn manner together with their Bibles. In this way the liturgy would become the real participation, here on earth and in time, of the nuptial celebration to which we are all invited.

This is how Sofia got us to work, those of us in our twenties and already in college, young people about 16 years old, and boys and girls around 12, all around the Bible. All together we formed a community of catechists during our Saturday afternoon Masses, and often we would also go out for pizza or to experience prayer with a community of cloistered sisters or with monks. Hence, on the day of their confirmation, those boys and girls surrounding the altar truly did guide the Mass, proclaim the Word of God, and meditate on it for themselves and for the adults, testifying that the Holy Spirit had descended over them.

Another of the important experiences linked to the center at Via degli Orsini were the various retreats led by Father Dalmazio Mongillo, a Dominican priest and professor of moral theology at the *Angelicum* (a theology university in Rome), who has been with us and continues to be with us in a special way in our work.

Our meetings with him were, in fact, foundational to a more profound understanding of morality, as he elucidated the true change of course happening within the Church's understanding of morality, which went from obedience and observance of norms in a rather formal and exterior manner, to a morality centered instead on conscience.

Father Mongillo taught us to welcome the meaning of life and not to desire to impose a meaning upon it ourselves. This understanding of morality based on wanting and remaining a part of the history in which each of us began our existence, but which did not start with us, is fundamentally what

Sofia and Gianna discovered when they designed the history strip to give children in the atrium.

Father Mongillo also touched on the sacrament of reconciliation, shedding light on a newly understood aspect of sin: that it is not necessarily a wicked action, but a "non-response" of love. He also commented on Pope John XXIII's encyclical *Peace on Earth* and helped us to enter into a more profound understanding of Eucharist as gift.

The depth of his meditation was a great help to us as catechists. In fact every gesture, every word, whether it was in the Bible or in the liturgy, assumed for us new meaning, which we would then compare among ourselves. So a word like *forgiveness,* whose meaning can retain for us a sense which impoverishes us and makes us passive (Who ever thought of resolving a conflict through forgiveness?), becomes "gift"—strength from God—"for" breaking the chains of injustice.

With boys and girls who were preparing for confirmation we would often start with the Bible, and then search in the liturgy, in order to discover new meaning about our place in history. With respect to this reality, we adults are often like people who have fallen asleep; children and young people draw us into fuller consciousness of the moment we are living in history and of the words of the Bible, which we read with them. How then can we fail to come to celebrate Easter in a manner that unites us to our roots, as Sofia has proposed, in order to arrive at the fullness to which we are called: "God all in all"?

This is my account of the many years in which I have shared, and continue to share, work and affection at the Center of Catechesis with Sofia and Gianna, years which have gotten me, as well as the other ex-children, into the habit of exacting, meticulous study, of searching out the essential, and of recognizing that we were created for great things.

Translated by Maureen Armas and Rebekah Rojcewicz

Memories of "a Big Girl Who Helps Sofia"

Francesca Cocchini

One day some children of the atrium on Via degli Orsini called me "a big girl who helps Sofia," and that is how I like to regard myself and to be regarded. Rather than narrate my experience in the atrium, an experience that began in 1960 when I was nine years old and continues without interruption to this day, first as a little girl and then as a catechist, I would like to open the eyes of my memory—which are the eyes of the heart—and describe what they see, recalling images, moments, events, and people's faces, then placing them on the timeline of my life's story, like a golden thread going through it.

Around a Table

Clearly, the first image that comes to mind in seeing myself as a little girl in the atrium is this: I am seated at the *round table* in the blue room (blue was the color of the tapestry in the room of the "grown-ups"), resting my elbows and waiting my turn to write down the names of some dear persons, "dead" or "alive," on small strips of paper. These strips would be inserted into appropriate frames and later read during Mass at the time of the memorial of the living and the dead. At that time, in the 1960s, Mass was celebrated in the atrium one Sunday a month, and we children were already doing many things, even though the liturgical reform had not yet come and the priest did not face us while celebrating Mass. Sofia would explain to us the meaning of the few gestures we were able to observe. I remember one in particular that we paid much attention to: At the time of the prayer called *"Orate, fratres,"* the priest made a complete 360° turn, not just a half turn of 180°, to indicate that this invitation to prayer was extended to the whole world. And at that moment it seemed to me like the whole world had entered the room, had entered the Mass, which thus became a truly cosmic Mass.

Also, around a *long table*—in this case the table in the room in front of the "chapel," a rectangular table that couldn't be moved by lifting, but only by dragging. I recall the many eucharistic celebrations we had there after the Council reform, when I was an adolescent and then a college student, and with a group made up of adults, young people, and children. We felt the desire to celebrate Mass according to the pace we set—extremely calm and participatory—because it was not enough for us to have the Masses that we prepared, every Sunday, in the church of the *Piazza del Popolo,* for a larger group of people and open to all who were passing by. I can still feel the intensity of not wanting to lose any of the richness of life being communicated in those more intimate celebrations. For this reason, we focused each time on a moment, a gesture, a prayer, but without losing sight of the unity. Indeed, the objective was always that of discovering how to unite the Liturgy of the Word with the Liturgy of the Eucharist. This challenge Sofia gave herself and us each time, and also, above all, the challenge of bringing "history" into the "liturgical rite." In those celebrations I began to experience the increasingly bright expectancy of the Second Coming, which we were preparing for, right there, at the very moment of our invocation.

Around that same *long table* I remember all the Eucharists celebrated with the children while I was a catechist. One of them left an indelible mark on me. During the prayer of thanksgiving, Marina, a little girl with serious disabilities, rose to her feet. As though inspired, she recited very slowly, almost syllable by syllable, from memory, the entire psalm of the Good Shepherd. I remember the intense silence of all the other children and of us catechists, a silence interrupted at the end by the solemn "Amen" proclaimed by Sofia.

Another *rectangular table,* with drawers, which is now in the room of the grown-ups, the central room of Sofia's house, emerges in my memory. At the time, this table was in the last room, which is now the little children's room. In that room there was only this one table, with many big chairs. Around that table for several years (from 1964 to, if I recall, 1968), Sofia organized special meetings for the postconfirmation children each Saturday afternoon. She had asked a professor from the Biblical Institute, Father Giovanni Rossetto, to initiate us into exegesis. I was the smallest one in the group and still hadn't learned Greek. Father Rossetto allowed me to take part with the others, as long as I didn't cause a disturbance by asking too many questions. And so I would listen, understanding very little, but the little I understood entered into me. It convinced me that the whole world of the Bible was a "very serious matter" and that my doubts and perplexities on the subject of faith were due to my ignorance, not to the triviality or insignificance of biblical data.

I can say that around that table, where we placed our Bibles and where we took notes—that's where I learned how to take notes!—I overcame my crises of faith as an adolescent. And great was my joy when, having now become a catechist with the children who were being prepared for confirmation, Sofia assigned me to a small group for two years. I would meet with this group right there in that room, around that table. And again, on top of that table, we opened our Bibles. . . . But we catechists—the same ones who years before had been involved in the "exegesis" adventure with the professor from the Biblical Institute—were meeting this time with Sofia every week, around another table, her *dining room table.* And there, Sofia prepared with us the subjects we were to present to the children. Once again the inseparable Bible–liturgy connection became an inexhaustible discovery, a source of contemplation and a strong stimulus to make us delve into history.

In those years, Sofia and Gianna had not yet "invented" the history strips; but when those strips appeared, they proved to be immediately familiar. Everything—the entire Bible, the entire liturgy—seemed to be just waiting to find its place in those strips. Or better, history and time became a "ribbon" to be extended, a roll of paper to be unrolled, which revealed to us a theological timeline, a mystery of Presence. Once again a level surface appears before me: It isn't really a *table,* but the green carpet on the floor that served as a *table,* because a lot of room is required to organize history or to organize the "Mass cards." Around this table, the carpet on the floor, we can all be together again, we the catechists and the children, to tell about our discoveries, to make a little more visible what is invisible.

Seated on a Chair

I remember Sofia as a religion teacher seated on a school *chair.* I was between 11 and 13 years old when I attended the experimental Montessori department of the *Virgilio* Middle School on Via Giulia. Sofia never stood at the desk, but she took a chair the way we did. (There were ten of us pupils.) She moved up close to the first bench, and there she opened the Bible and began telling us about the parables. I hadn't attended classes in the atrium as a little girl, and so for me this was something completely new. One recollection stands out among so many: the parable of the ten virgins. After the meditation, I wanted to draw a picture of this parable. Being very interested in the story, I drew next to the bridegroom a picture of a bride. When I brought the drawing to Sofia, she pointed out to me that the text says nothing about a bride. I was taken aback and felt a bit ashamed at letting myself be carried away by the drawing instead of being faithful to the text. But Sofia said to me: "And yet, if there is a bridegroom there should also be a bride. Who could she be?" It was then I discovered with incredible amazement that in the kingdom of heaven each one of us is called to be a "bride," a partner of the spousal covenant, in love with an "everlasting and very special love." And there, at the *Virgilio* Middle School in the Montessori department, at the age of 13, I "discovered" the newborn and the "little child," guided by the wisdom of Gianna Gobbi. One day, Gianna brought all of us, boys and girls, to the "Children's House" in *Palazzo Taverna,* where we met Miss Costa Gnocchi. She had us stay there one whole morning, sitting on little *chairs* to "observe" how a child should be respected. Then, in the classroom, she taught us how to work with materials—with our hands—so that the hand could become the docile instrument of intelligence.

Still seated on a *chair,* I can see myself in the large room on the top floor of the vicariate, where Sofia and Gianna had been called to give courses for catechists. Up till then, the courses had been organized more "informally" on Via degli Orsini. I, too, was learning how to be a catechist, but I often had to take my seat and place it next to that of Sofia behind a long table, with a sea of people in front of us—almost all nuns from the most varied institutes. What was I doing beside Sofia? I simply had to read the biblical texts that Sofia would comment on, so as to help save her voice. Otherwise, in that big room it would have soon failed her. But the reading was not continuous. Sofia interrupted me at almost every verse. And so, in this way, I learned that in scripture actually "no word of the text is superfluous and without meaning," that "scripture is interpreted with scripture," and that the Word of God is like a chisel which, chipping away at a rock, makes a lot of sparks. In fact, "every word that comes from the mouth of the Holy One"—as the school of Rabbi Ishmael teaches—"is translated into 70 languages and is capable of 70 interpretations." Seated next to Sofia, while reading the Bible I learned how to read the Bible. And later, as a grown-up, when I studied the Fathers of the Church and became familiar with their writings, I discovered in them that same hermeneutic method that has been for me, and continues to be, a source of great joy, a guarantee of truth and faithfulness.

But to see myself seated on a chair is, for me, above all, to see myself in the atrium with the children. During my first year as a catechist at the Parish of Our Lady of Lourdes, to prepare myself for the meetings with the children, I went on the first day to the atrium on Via degli Orsini to observe how it was done. I sat down on a *very small chair* and made myself as small as I could in order not to disturb anyone. Then, at the end, Gianna made me note down everything that had escaped me, and she explained to me the meaning of what I had noted. After that day, the more experience I had with my groups, the more I remained seated. And now I'm very pleased when, in a meeting with the children, I can stay seated a long time on a *chair* in a corner next to the door, to contemplate their way of working: at times individually, at times in twos or threes, more often in silence, but sometimes with a bit of "chatterboxing," which (unless it is disturbing) I prefer not to interrupt, not even when every once in a while it has to do with things different from what we are working on, for it is a sign of freedom. It indicates that the children feel at ease, and I think in this way they can better understand that all their lived experience is bound up in a relationship with God. And when a child calls me, I like to take a chair next to that child. It seems to me in this way we are more together in seeking the same Source, in listening to the same Master.

And in the atrium on Via degli Orsini, or rather, in Sofia's study—which is not part of the atrium as such, except on special occasions, and the one I mention now is one of those occasions—there is a *small armchair* which, in certain meetings in preparation for First Communion, is moved into a corner and surrounded by as many children's chairs as there are children. While seated there, Sofia always talked about the parable of the "True Vine." And it was sitting there that, one year, I had to give this talk, because Sofia was away in Israel. I recall the intense emotion, and the apprehension of Augusta who was overseeing that everything was in order and that everything took place "the way it did when Miss Sofia was there." Above all, I remember the looks of the children, looks that, once again, did nothing but rise and fall continually on the Gospels placed on their knees.

But certainly, the best time spent while seated on a *chair* was on the Sunday afternoons of each year, at the close of the First Communion retreat. Every year the same miracle takes place: The children begin to work again with practically nothing—during the days of retreat, they do drawings, copying, and readings from the Gospel. They are at peace, calm, humming, untiring in their enjoyment; and we the catechists remain seated, encouraged by their extraordinary earnestness.

As you can well imagine, I could go on and on. But I prefer to end in this way, simply and full of gratitude.

Translated by Father Joseph Occhio, SDB

I Leave My Heart Here

Patricia Coulter

Jesus rejoiced in the Holy Spirit . . . (Luke 10:21)

What encourages me to offer the following bits and pieces is a story Sofia Cavalletti told me during my first stay in Rome, from 1975 to 1977. It was about an experience she had as a young child, when she was around age five. She wanted a way to express her gratitude to her mother for teaching her how to read. For Sofia, the ability to read was the best gift possible and brought utter liberation, which she prized beyond valuation. She wanted to thank her mother, but how? What did she have to give to her mother that could compare with such a gift? Sofia searched through her belongings to find all the money she had. She took these four coins—Sofia remembers their number and value exactly because they represented her entire fortune at that time—and gave them all to her mother as a thank you gift.

In this spirit of thanksgiving, I offer a few of the moments of meeting and conversation with Sofia Cavalletti and Gianna Gobbi, and with some of their closest companions.

Sofia

My first meeting with Sofia was by mail and was the fruit of a retreat I made during Holy Week in 1975, while on Easter break from the Montessori school where I was working at the time. I went to celebrate the Easter Triduum at a Benedictine monastery of contemplative women and had brought a sense of inner restlessness. Personally, I found myself at a crossroads and wanted to know God more concretely. My professional dissatisfaction was familiar to me; years earlier, the same impulse had led me from traditional teaching to study at the Montessori College in Dublin, Ireland. Now, after having taught in three Montessori schools, discontent surfaced again, taking the form of a new question: But what about Maria Montessori's vision concerning the spiritual formation of children? With whom could I explore this reality? Montessori had written, in *The Child in the Church* (edited by E. M. Standing), of her initiatives to help children live life with Christ in the rhythm of the liturgical year and in the sacraments. That book also contained contributions from persons who had continued this work in various ways.

During this retreat, my longing and discontent opened onto a new horizon. To describe this moment, I find myself returning to a phrase I would hear later, after I had met Sofia: "Life is a passage from the less to the more." Sofia used this phrase to describe the movement of God, revealed so powerfully in the Gospel parables, especially in the parables of the mustard seed and the leaven (Matthew 13).

Of the various contributions to *The Child in the Church,* the most compelling was Sofia's chapter, in which she described the experience that she and Gianna had developed in their catechetical center in Rome. Taking a step toward that new horizon, I found Sofia's address and wrote her a letter.

Sofia remembers that in my first letter to her I said I wanted to study liturgy with her. In her return letter, she clarified, "I am not a liturgist." She laughs when she recalls this exchange. Her light-hearted refusal to ascribe to herself what she believes does not belong to her is an attitude I have come to know well. She also resists claiming authorship—either literally or metaphorically—for what she does not deem to be hers or hers alone. I remember two things about her response to my letter: her openness and an invitation. She said that I was welcome to come and study with her in Rome. But then she said that since she would be traveling that summer to the Americas for the first time, to give a course at a Montessori center directed by A. M. Joosten in St. Paul, Minnesota, why not come and see?

And so in July of 1975 I arrived in St. Paul on a Saturday, a few days before Sofia's course was to begin, to hear the closing address Sofia would give that night at a Montessori conference. What Sofia remembers from our first face-to-face meeting is that I asked, "What shall I call you?" Until that time, I had been accustomed, in university and Montessori studies, to using surnames; depending on the education of the individual, the surname might be prefaced with other titles, such as professor or doctor. My intuition told me that the person before me had more titles than anyone I had yet encountered. Sofia finds it amusing to recall my first words to her, as though she had simply assumed that I would have done as she invited me to do that day and call her "Sofia."

Sofia's invitation to use her first name marked the beginning, for me, of a new way of learning. In their center of catechesis in Rome, I later discovered that the children call all the adults by name. Now I perceive a symbolic meaning in this practice. God calls us all, old and young, into a relationship of covenant; in fact, Jesus held up the child as the example for the rest of us. In light of the mystery of this covenant relationship, titles of any kind become insignificant.

On the evening of the day when I met Sofia, she addressed the Montessori convocation in St. Paul. Of the many words she said that evening, I vividly remember one phrase: "No child has ever been loved enough," in the family, within the community. Sofia's phrase expressed her insight into the child's essential hunger and capacity for relationship with God, but even more, her words pointed to the essential nature of God, who does love enough, whose love is always enough. "God is love. Jesus is risen!" was the fundamental proclamation that would become the key motif which echoed throughout all the scriptural and liturgical themes Sofia presented during that course. As this revelation developed and deepened throughout the following weeks, the transforming power of God's love resounded deeply within me.

Since that time, in my years using this catechesis, I have had the privilege to observe the same transformation in others too. Recently, two women responded to Sofia's second volume of *The Religious Potential of the Child*. One, a woman of mature years and rich in life experience, exclaimed, "I'm in love!" She added, "It's not new. I knew it before. But. . . ." Her voice trailed off into silence. The other, a mother of young children and catechist in her large Polish-speaking parish, struggled to find the words in English: "It goes into me . . . deep . . . into my heart . . . and makes me so happy." She borrowed my copy of the book and found the passage that had touched her: "Liturgy recharges us, giving us the energy we need to live as children of light and to work toward its fullest possible shining" (111–12). Her whole face shone as she read these words.

I wrote to Sofia about the response of these two women, recalling the words of Maria Montessori, "The child's soul is like a mirror on which every breath is registered." I suggested to Sofia that her book offers a view, full of reverence and humility, into the child's soul, and I asked her whether it is possible that the child can mirror to us a glimpse of the immense value and beauty of our own ageless and eternal soul. She wrote to me in response:

Christmas 2002

Yes, I am also convinced of the great impact that this catechesis has on adults; it is one of the most beautiful surprises that this catechesis gifts us with. How many letters come to me confirming what you say. I believe, however, that a resonance such as this in adults contains a particular aspect: the presence, the action of the child, because of which the Christian message acquires a different voice, a voice that is "silent and light," like the sound that Elijah heard on Mount Horeb, and at the same time the voice is such that it is heard and it is discerned beyond the thundering of the tempest, the earthquake, etc. It is the voice of a particular teacher: a teacher who teaches without knowing it, and without those who are listening being aware that they are in the presence of one who is teaching them.

I believe that this chance to listen is the particular privilege of all of us who are catechists of the Good Shepherd; this is the gift, which we must become more clearly conscious of in this time of the feast of the GIFT, so that we can be—I do not say sufficiently grateful, because this will never be possible—but so that we will be more able to savor and enjoy it.

I arrived in Rome in the fall of 1975 to study at the center of catechesis, located in Sofia's home on Via degli Orsini. "Children really do live in a different religious world; it is hard for us to understand just how different," Sofia would later say during the course she gave on Bible and liturgy. This period of study was an introduction to a new world of paradox: in which the littlest are the greatest and in which the least are the wisest in the ways of the kingdom. In this world the child is a parable.

At the same time, I was introduced to life in a children's atrium, which is a concrete expression of this paradoxical world. I discovered, for example, that the atrium is a place where adults can be schooled in the Christian life by children who are viewed as master teachers.

I think of this rich new world I discovered in Sofia's home as a series of widening, interconnected circles of relationships and activities. At its core, around which all activities and interests orbit, is the loving God of the covenant. Very close to this core, and radiating from it, is the life of the atrium, where the children live and celebrate their relationship with God. Children of different ages have been coming for 50 years, two hours each week, to an area in Sofia's home, which has been permanently put at the disposal of the children. There are three atrium rooms, with high ceilings and windows along one wall. God is the fire, the *focolare* of Sofia's home, and she has given the children a place closest to the hearth. Surrounding this essential work with children, a circle of adults, Sofia and Gianna principal among them, have served as guides in the formation of those adults who come to the weekly course sessions. Many other circles of relationship radiate from this circle.

All the adults I encountered at this center had God as a common focus, and all had chosen to serve children. These adults form a womb-like community, reminiscent of the people of Israel, called to wait, watch for, and receive the Messiah. Sofia and Gianna, along with their collaborators, have themselves been welcoming and receptive to those being born into relationship with God. The atrium materials, which the adults have crafted, express and manifest a welcoming attitude; the atrium space is a physical, external sign of this receptivity.

While I was in Rome, the space was laid out as follows: One room, at the farthest end of the house, was where the weekly course for adults was held. Beside this room was the atrium for the "little ones," children six and under, where Gianna was the catechist. The atrium for children around six to nine years of age adjoined this one. Through a doorway was a fourth space that opened into a hallway and had an adjoining room, tiny and chapel-like. The older children gathered in this final room.

Time spent in the atrium allowed me to witness a certain way of being present to children. While participating in a meeting of catechists and educators, who all shared a passion for fostering and exploring the religious life of children, Tilde Cocchini, one of Sofia's and Gianna's closest collaborators, related an experience, which typifies this new way of being present. As Tilde described this experience, she reflected on what had happened and wished to hear the responses of those listening. As she began her account, I found myself writing down everything she said because there was something dynamic about the way Tilde recounted the conversation she had had with the young atrium children. She was able to provide such depth of detail, to give her initial and then later insights about the exchange. As she spoke, she expressed a profound awareness of the subtlest movements within the children. She seemed to catch every nuance of tone in the children's voices. She was even able to describe the length of the silences that occurred during the children's meditation.

In Tilde's atrium in Our Lady of Lourdes Parish in Rome, while presenting the parable of the Good Shepherd to a newly arrived group of young children (under six), the following exchange took place between Tilde and the children:

> "And who is the Good Shepherd?" asked Tilde after the solemn reading of Jesus' parable of the Good Shepherd (John 10). All the children responded that he was Jesus. She then asked, "And these sheep who are so loved by Jesus?" No one responded. "Are they like the sheep we see in the fields, for example? Or are they different?" Again, no response. "Who are the sheep . . . ?"
>
> Then the new boy, Alessandro, who was 3 years, 2 months old, said, *sottovoce,* "Me."
>
> All the children were silent.
>
> "It's true," said Tilde, "You are a sheep."
>
> "No, I'm not a sheep," said the boy. "I am Alessandro."
>
> Another silence followed these words.
>
> Then a 5-year-old girl said, with great longing, "I would like to be a sheep."
>
> "Me too," said another child.
>
> "Me too," said Tilde.
>
> Tilde did not pursue the question further.

Tilde spoke to our group of the moment in which Alessandro whispered, "Me." She felt as though the Holy Spirit had spoken in him. It almost seemed, by his later response, that he was unaware that he had said the word *me.* She also spoke of the supreme delicacy needed to allow children to pray as they are, not to move, impede, or precipitate their discovery. She felt amazed at how close the children had come to understanding their identity as sheep, and at how the children had expressed such great longing to be the object of the Good Shepherd's immense love. Tilde found it remarkable that the children did not feel it was disharmonious that sheep should be so loved by Jesus. They accepted that Christ would demonstrate a sort of cosmic loving kindness toward all creation.

I reflected many years before I found a name for this quality, that Tilde and Gianna each manifested in their relationships with adults and children, and which Sofia also embodies. They are spiritual companions. They are catechists who have practiced, each in her own way, the respectful attentiveness required to allow children their own personal discovery of the covenant relationship. To be a catechist means to share in their sensitivity, patience, and deep reverence for the movement of the Holy Spirit in the soul . . . of a three-year-old.

Gianna

Only days after I arrived at the center in Rome, I met Gianna Gobbi. Right away, in that joyful enthusiasm that was characteristic of her, Gianna promised that when I learned to speak Italian we would read the parable of the Good Shepherd together. A happy prospect! So too was her offer to help me explore the Montessori dimension of the catechesis, and to bring me to visit the *Centro Nascita,* a Montessori center for pregnant women and infants.

By the spring of that year, my Italian had improved to the point where I could understand Gianna without an interpreter. She invited me to her home, where we spent the morning in a conversation that ranged over many topics. She spoke of her interest in setting up a sort of laboratory for the development of the materials. She envisioned an experimental center where people could go to work with their heads and their hands. She expressed her wish to work further on the Old Testament materials, and to rework materials that had been developed in the past but were no longer in use. As well, Gianna shared her desire to form an association, to develop a newsletter, and to help the catechetical work grow in a new direction. She also discussed her wish to create a "model album," and the necessity of remaining open to combining the Montessori method with religions in general and not only Catholicism.

In that same conversation, Gianna offered some of her personal story. She shared that her grandmother's family was from the same region in Italy as part of Maria Montessori's family. She spoke of her experience during World War II and of her need, at that time, to take her Montessori training clandestinely under the fascist government. She confided that she thought Anna Maria Maccheroni, with whom Gianna had worked, was very nearly the cofounder of Montessori's work in the realm of the spiritual development of children. Gianna was of the opinion that Montessori, with whom Gianna had also worked, had promoted a science of the true nature of the human person, and that her genius lay in her deeply held belief that the child was truly created in the image of God.

In speaking about the prehistory of the Catechesis of the Good Shepherd, Gianna described her work with younger children, in Adele

Costa Gnocchi's school. It was Costa Gnocchi who had suggested that Gianna and Sofia meet, saying, "Sofia knows everything about scripture! And you know the child."

Gianna and Sofia met in 1954. Gianna explained that together they developed ideas, experimented with materials, and observed the children's responses. At that time, however, they did not understand the significance of the richness they experienced in their encounters with the children. Gianna felt as if they had added two plus two and had found that the sum was 22, the results were that much greater than the effort they had put into the work.

In recalling this experience, Gianna thought that trying to develop materials or presentations apart from a living atrium experience could become deadening. She cautioned that catechesis can become "intellectual-ized" in the absence of children who choose materials and themes according to their needs. Our conversation ended that day with Gianna expressing her conviction that "the Holy Spirit dwells without resistance in children."

Chief among Gianna's many gifts were her ability to observe and her talent for working and living in community. In her, each of these gifts might be more accurately characterized as a charism.

Gianna had a watchful heart and an attentive spirit. She always noticed others and viewed them as sacred. Observation was a spiritual practice, and one that she prized in the formation of those who accompany the inner life of the child. She wrote in a letter:

3 December 1992

I looked at the program you sent [an outline for an adult formation program in the Catechesis of the Good Shepherd that she and Sofia had been working on with me], which Sofia showed me. Unfortunately, I am not able to study it as I would like because of the language; for what I manage to understand, it is a valuable work. Do not forget, in the preparation of catechists, the importance of their capacity to be observers of the child and respectful of the secret (of childhood). This aspect must complete the formation of those who put themselves beside the child, and even more so of those who initiate and help the child in the knowledge of God and in a relationship with Him.

Similarly, community was of great importance in Gianna's life and work. This was reflected in a letter she wrote in May 2001, following a recent assembly of the executive committee of the International Council. Her vision for this gathering was that it might bring about "unity in diversity and help the young ones (adults new to this method of catechesis) in a precious work." She continued:

> As you will have seen by the report of the meeting, . . . the changes are noteworthy. Organization is not the final goal, but rather to spread the work, and to lessen the direct action of Sofia. It is necessary that a shape be found, a structure of support, and this report is an attempt. No one will be able to substitute for Sofia, we know this, and so it is necessary to have a group to whom reference can be made, so that the work is supported in its future.

These words testify to Gianna's commitment and faith in the strength of community. She closed the letter with three terms that sum up what she held closest to her heart: ". . . the Christian message, our Church, the Child."

What Gianna had remarked as Montessori's most important talent was also her own; she too believed that the child was created in the image of God. I feel it was for this reason that Gianna always capitalized the first letter in the word *child*. And to Gianna, all adults were also children at heart; this conviction animated and informed her gift for community.

Despite all her experience, the fecundity of her thought, and her charisma, she never called herself a teacher. She always stressed that the only teacher is Christ, who taught that the littlest children are the most wise (Matthew 11:25). Gianna allowed Jesus, through the work and words of the children in the atrium, to teach her. In fact, during our first meeting, Gianna told me, "Do not take me as an example." Her humility was the greatest gift she possessed and the ground out of which all her other gifts grew.

Final Reflection

One day during my stay in Rome, Sofia invited a Dominican priest, Father Dalmazio Mongillo, to her home for a conversation. Several other catechists were present. Sofia had a question for Father Mongillo regarding what he had written in an introduction to her first volume of *The Religious Potential of the Child.* While the finer points of the discussion escape my memory, I vividly recall the vivacity and honesty of their exchange. Sofia was concerned that Father Mongillo had credited Sofia and Gianna themselves for the work they had initiated 21 years earlier. Sofia maintained that the fruits of this long journey with the children could not be ascribed to her. As Father Mongillo was leaving, he said to me, "They think it's all about the materials." He smiled gently as if to suggest that Sofia and Gianna might be overlooking the obvious, then said, "But it's them." Although I agreed that the materials serve a most significant role in this catechesis, I understood what he meant and secretly sided with him.

Since then, two phrases have helped me to understand better Sofia's, Gianna's, and Tilde's impulse to attribute all the fruitfulness of their work to God and to the child. The first phrase is an insight Father Mongillo offered to me more recently. He said, "Do you realize that none of us ever sees our own face? We always and only see ourselves as mirrored," literally or figuratively in the face before us. The other phrase was a question, posed by a child. A four-year-old girl, while washing her hands before dinner, was unperturbed when asked to hurry. The steaming-hot feast had already been laid out, awaiting her arrival. As she slowly soaked her hands in the water, her thoughts were intent on something. Then she looked up and asked, "Do you know who has love in their eyes?" She had been thinking of the persons she loved, who loved her; then she began to name them, in answer to her own question.

These two statements helped me to appreciate that Sofia and Gianna could not see what they were mirroring back to the children whom they were companioning, but the children could see the love shining from Sofia's and Gianna's eyes. One simple example that captures this has returned to memory during the process of writing this essay. During my first visit in Rome, at the close of a session in the atrium for the older children, a girl about nine years of age was readying to leave. She walked across the room to bid her good-bye to Sofia, but she appeared reluctant to go. As they looked at one another, the girl moved her hand to her heart, then placed it in Sofia's hands, and said, "I'm going now, but I leave my heart here."

Gianna

Sofia Cavalletti

W hy is it so difficult for me to write about Gianna when we have
spent almost half a century united by friendship and by work?
When people ask me about her, when I take up my pen to write
about her, I seem to remember nothing. And yet I feel her always so close to
me, to the point that I overflow with joy when I see a person who might
look like her in some way, and I continuously think, "I must tell this to
Gianna," or "I have to show this to Gianna."

In order to be able to speak about her, I must begin from afar, finish-
ing, perhaps, where I should begin. My memory of Gianna cannot be separated from her beautiful country house. These words must not make you
think of a luxurious villa. I would like to underline the words *beautiful* and
countryside. Gianna's house was beautiful because it had kept all of its rustic character. The countryside made it so beautiful and special.

The fields did not only surround it, but they seemed to creep into it
through the doors and through every window (maybe they also penetrated
through the walls). Every breeze brought in with it the soul of the fields,
autumn fields the plow was preparing for the seed, or spring or summer
fields wrapped with so many colors. And yet around the house there was
quite a large space covered with gravel where if a weed tried to push up, it
was immediately plucked out by the inexorable hoe of Gianna's sister,
Natalia, or by Gianna herself.

Gianna's house had kept, within itself, the different aspects of the
fields: the festive aspect of the mature fields and, at the same time, the
roughness that they present after being plowed. Once, when Gianna came
back to Rome after a brief spring country sojourn, I asked her, "How was
the countryside?" She answered, "A bride!"

Gianna's passion for the country was not a romantic one. It was akin
to the spirit of the Latin poet, Virgil, as expressed, not in his pastoral poem,
the *Eclogues,* but in the poem dedicated to work in the fields, the *Georgics.*

Even the hospitality in Gianna's house had a special character. I do
not want you to misunderstand it if I say it was rustic. With this word I want

to express sincere cordiality, true simplicity, and the capacity to offer up for enjoyment the different aspects of the seasons.

Here and there in the house, sunflowers gave back some of the sunshine they had drunk in the fields. During the vintage, the most beautiful clusters of grapes, together with some leaves, brought the beauty of the vine all the way to the center of the dining table, which was enriched with the luxury of its colors.

Gianna's hospitality has never made me feel like a guest. She allowed me to divide my time between the hours spent with her and a time of solitude, when books often remained closed, because the attraction of the spectacle of the fields was too strong and made it impossible to divert my eyes from it. How many hours did I spend looking, spellbound, at the plowed fields—so severe, so coarse, so stark, so naked and poor, and so full of hope.

What shall I say about the wonderful sunsets, in which it seemed that a great painter had used all the shades of his palette! These sunsets set the barn afire like a flaring torch; with its few, small, and blocked windows, the barn seemed not to realize the beauty of the transformation that the sunset was working on its bricks, offering this beauty with generosity to anyone who looked at it. At the same time, the house stood by quietly with its doors and windows thrown open.

When the day ended, two other shows awaited us. If it was a cool night, a great blazing fireplace *(focolare)* dominated the wider ground-floor room, as it did in all the peasants' houses. Or we would stroll under the stars while Gianna tried to recognize the constellations and to remember their names.

That countryside and that house had an important part in Gianna's life. She had reconquered the house little by little, rescuing it from the tenant farmers, to whom she gave land in exchange. To furnish the house, Gianna had set in motion all of her capacity for fantasy—the fantasy life for which I called her "Moritz." Moritz was a character in the *Corriere dei Piccoli,* a little journal for children I read when I was young; he was always undertaking extraordinary projects which, contrary to those of Gianna, always ended in disasters. Gianna was capable of transforming an old object full of dust, more or less shapeless, discovered someplace, into a little table, or a stool, or a shelf, or some other thing with which she could furnish the various rooms of her house. If she saw something in an old storeroom or market, that to me looked absolutely useless, immediately, the wheels of Moritz's brain would begin spinning and find an ingenious use for it. Gianna accomplished her projects with the ant's philosophy: little by little. Her drawers were full of drawings of things fermenting in her head.

The countryside was both Gianna's cross and her delight. Bureaucratic complications gave her frequent headaches, but the headaches were greatly outweighed by her joy in every rose that bloomed, the mushrooms we would look for in the morning under the poplar trees, and above all, by the summer harvest. On these occasions, all of Gianna's "peasant" soul emerged. Gianna was always a cricket who moved quickly from one place to the other, often disappearing unexpectedly out of sight of her companions, but when the farm machines arrived for the harvest, the rapidity of her movements multiplied! She could be standing beside you, but the next moment you would see her as a tiny, tiny speck on the far side of the field or climbing a tractor. At night, she came back covered with dust, but very happy at having taken to the farmers' cooperative what the fields had given after the winter's sleep.

This quickness of movement earned her another nickname, "Little Mouse." The irony is that Gianna was in a continuous state of open warfare with mice, which made her invent the most mouse-icidal traps. In spite of this fact, some courageous mice would dare to dart out before her eyes. These mice aroused Gianna, more than ever, to mouse-icidal rages.

I have spoken of Gianna's countryside, because Gianna lived in relation to it with a spirit that I would define as religious. It is not possible to separate the peasant Gianna from the researcher and Montessori educator. In her, the soul of the educator and the soul of the "peasant" were combined in perfect unity, and both constituted her person.

The seasonal rhythms of the countryside entered into Gianna and forged in her the discipline she brought to her work as an educator. The countryside rhythms impose a discipline because they cannot be rushed but require you to wait patiently; they do not allow you to pretend, for example, that a geranium flowers out of season. Gianna had learned very well how to wait. Her "peasant" patience was linked in an absolutely natural way with her Montessorian attitude, an attitude that wishes the educator to know and respect the time of each child's maturation. As Gianna watched the slow changes in nature, she also knew how to watch, without attempting to hasten, the slow normalization of the child and his or her manifestation as a child of God. Gianna's knowing how to wait was the expression of a deep respect—a religious respect—in front of the manifestations of the miracle of life, in all its forms.

For us, Gianna's beautiful house was also a place of work. There, usually under the shadow of one of the mulberry trees, we reviewed the entire second volume of *The Religious Potential of the Child* together. I called this place "my belvedere," because from there a wide view opened on the Marches countryside that is so serene, so mild, and so "caressed" by the hands of man. In that beautiful countryside, the colors faded until they reached the mountains. Sometimes, depending on the weather, we worked in that enjoyable place we called the hut *(capanna),* where the peasant atmosphere was made more evident by the presence of some farm tools and the big and small baskets that hung from the eaves ready to receive the white and black figs and the peaches that came from the trees growing in the vineyard. Maybe the peaches didn't look very nice, but they compensated with a wonderful perfume and a genuine flavor, which we no longer know in the cities. In the hut, the horizon was not as broad as the one we could see from my belvedere under the tree, but a gentle breeze blew in. In that place, which I also sometimes called, with a certain irony, *il roseto* (the rose garden) *delle Marche,* the roses peered in at the little windows and, together with the roses that Gianna had set on the table, delighted our eyes and inspired the little touches that the book's second volume required.

Several of our strips have been laid out on Gianna's bed, in front of the three open windows of her room invaded by the sun. In the feast of light of that room, we examined them, we reviewed them, we discussed them, and we declared them ready . . . for the next revision.

If we get to talking about work, it is more difficult for me to talk about Gianna. Her presence, her collaboration, is so familiar, so taken for granted. Everything was so intertwined between us. As an ex-little atrium girl said at Gianna's funeral, "In my memory, it was Gianna's work to take the children by the hand and lead them to the Word of God, while Sofia brought the Word of God to the children." In every material that I look at, I see Gianna's pencils and pens, and also my saws. There is no material that was only her work or only mine. This intertwining, so evident and visible in the atrium, corresponds to an intertwining of feelings, of agreements, of passions, that our relation created between us. I will never be grateful enough to Gianna for this friendship, and to Adele Costa Gnocchi, who made us meet. From this description you can understand the void that Gianna's absence has left in my life; a part of me was taken away with her death. You can also understand that, at least for now, I cannot write longer.

June 7, 2002

Mysterious Growth

Tina Lillig

> This is what the kingdom of God is like. A person scatters seed on the
> ground. Night and day, while sleeping and while awake, the seed is
> sprouting and growing; how, he does not know. Of its own accord the
> earth produces, first the stalk, then the ear, then the full grain in the ear.
> (Mark 4:26–28)

Sleeping and rising, growing but not knowing how, producing of itself—
this scriptural wording could be used to characterize life lived with
children. Mark's short parable of the kingdom is certainly about mystery and about something small. It begins with simple human work, work
that starts a process which seems to continue without much human agency.

The parable in many ways and on many levels also seems to describe
the Catechesis of the Good Shepherd, which has been causing considerable
amazement among parents, catechists, parishes, and dioceses throughout
the United States. While this approach is radically child-led, it encompasses
all the themes most essential to the Christian message. This catechesis
allows God to speak directly to even the youngest child through scripture,
liturgy, and the mystery of life.

Beginnings

Though the Catechesis of the Good Shepherd began in Rome in 1954, it
did not arrive in North America until 1975 when Sofia Cavalletti gave a
course for adults in St. Paul, Minnesota. Sofia had discovered her work with
children quite by accident. A mother requested that Sofia give some religious instruction to her seven-year-old son. Refusing at first, she later consented, and the experience altered the course of her life. She saw in that
child, and in numerous other children since, a way of being in the presence
of God that is unique to the child. It is a way marked by quiet joy, satisfaction, and contemplative activity.

From the earliest days Sofia was joined by Gianna Gobbi, whose
expertise was the educational method of Maria Montessori. Together they

established an atrium, a room prepared for children that contains simple handmade materials for the child to use. The word *atrium* was borrowed from Montessori herself, who had used it when she began some religious work with children in Spain. It is an ancient word for the entry porch of a basilica where catechumens were prepared for Christian initiation.

The slow development of the hands-on materials that invite children into contemplative activity began in that first atrium in Rome. There children could ponder a biblical passage or a moment from the liturgy by taking the related material and working with it—placing wood figures of sheep in a sheepfold of the Good Shepherd, setting sculpted apostles around a Last Supper table, or preparing a small altar with furnishings used for the Eucharist. Older children who are able to read could copy the biblical sayings of Jesus, lay in order the written prayers from the rite of Baptism, or label a long timeline depicting the history of the kingdom of God.

At the root of the whole enterprise of the Catechesis of the Good Shepherd is the continuous evidence that God and the child are already in relationship and that children possess a unique capacity to respond to God's loving initiative. For five decades Sofia and Gianna collected, and Sofia continues to collect, this evidence, and out of it they have fashioned the contents of the atrium. This evidence appears in the form of the children's drawings, briefly worded insights, prayers, and joyful, prolonged, and repeated work with certain materials. The materials that the children ignored were weeded out, and what was left became a curriculum of sorts. Over the years these two founding mothers were astounded to discover that the children, by themselves, had selected the core of Christian belief, omitting nothing that was essential.

On walking into any atrium it is clear that the child, rather than the adult, is central. Every object is the right size for the children being served in that room. Art is hung at child-eye level. Objects and even chairs can be easily carried by children. In this way the catechist "decreases" so God and the child can meet.

A keen observer may also notice that the atrium gently invites children into a communal life. There is only one of each material, offering children a valuable dilemma: "I want to work with this material, but another child does too." Times of silence require that everyone work together to make the silence: "If just one person isn't working, we don't have silence." Chairs are set down two legs at a time, so as not to disturb the work of others. Pencils are sharpened way down before they are discarded to high-light the value of each thing. Prayer in common is a regular practice.

The Announcement

Striking, though not surprising, is the priority given to the Bible. As a biblical text is proclaimed in the atrium, it is seen as a living source of God's self revelation. "I wonder what God wants to tell us in this parable," is a common reflection of the catechist as the response of the children unfolds. Mark Searle, in his introduction to Sofia's book *The Religious Potential of the Child,* which has become a classic for religious educators, wrote: "It is . . . as refreshing as it is rare to find someone trained as a biblical scholar returning the Bible to the church as the living word of God and thus to be set alongside liturgy and life experience as a place of encounter with God" (Cavalletti, 1992, 4).

Even so, this catechesis takes great care to respect the historical character and literary genre of each scriptural passage presented to children. Before an infancy narrative such as the Annunciation, the Visitation, or the Presentation in the Temple, is offered to even three-year-olds, it is carefully prepared for with the biblical geography that illuminates it. And so a relief map with movable markers for cities has a dove marking Nazareth, a star for Bethlehem, and a cross for Jerusalem. There is a puzzle map of the Holy Land's regions and bodies of water, and older children mark many cities on a map with tiny pin labels. A model of the city of Jerusalem allows the sites of Holy Week to be named and placed.

The children's introduction to the Hebrew Scriptures is slow, consisting only of prophecies until the age of nine, prophecies that offer images for meditation (light, Isaiah 9:2; names, Isaiah 9:6; star and scepter, Numbers 24:17; etc.). Between nine and twelve the children can grasp and appreciate hidden truths, the force of culture, and the progressiveness of divine pedagogy (*General Directory for Catechesis,* 143). Together with their catechist they read, in rabbinical fashion, numerous texts that tell of the events of the history of salvation—creation, the fall, the flood, Abraham, Moses, the prophets. The selection of texts is precise, favoring those that either identify biblical ancestors as persons of their time and culture or that are reflected today in the liturgical rites of the Church. Thus, in order to identify Abraham as a true semi-nomad from ancient Sumer, not unfamiliar with ritual sacrifice, the children ponder the stories of his separation from Lot, the apparition at Mamre, and God's promise of land and descendants. The creation accounts and the episodes of the Exodus will echo again for them in the blessing of the baptismal water.

Indeed, liturgy shares equal priority with the Bible as "living source" of God in this catechesis. From the threshold of the atrium the tiniest child sees many objects similar to those in the church sanctuary usually glimpsed from a great distance. Through these objects, liturgical signs will become known and loved and will convey the hidden reality they hold. Gestures will be performed and meditated on in the atrium—*epiclesis,* offering, peace, *lavabo,* mingling of water and wine, genuflection, the sign of the cross. Through the baptismal candle, the white garment, the Gospel, and the oils, children will come to see the risen life of Christ that is shared in Baptism. As the children grow, full rites, including all the prayers, are meditated on and sometimes even copied. Many details are striking to the older child including the discovery, in probing the Eucharistic Prayers, of all those present at the Eucharist that we do not see with our eyes: the universal Church, the world, the dead, the heavenly Church.

The Catechesis of the Good Shepherd has kerygma as its starting point rather than doctrine or experience. It is not fashioned at a desk to include long lists of doctrinal elements. And yet those who practice it find a great richness of doctrine in the course of nine years of presentations (over one hundred fifty in number). Even the littlest ones absorb Catholic doctrine effortlessly. This is illustrated by four-year-old Micah who, after the presentation of the Visitation, traced figures of Mary and Elizabeth. Then he used a red pen and drew a figure around Mary. When asked about this figure, he said, "It is God surrounding Mary."

Unlike the most prevalent catechetical process that begins by helping children recall a common life experience, the catechist might begin by introducing, in the most objective manner possible, a biblical text or by using introductory words such as "When we go to the Eucharist we see, . . . we hear. . . ." Central to each presentation is the solemn reading of the text. A candle is lit before the scripture is read. Or a small table is prepared with cloth, plate, and cup, after which the catechist might read, "And so, Father, we bring you these gifts. We ask you to make them holy. . . ." The children reflect on what they have just seen and heard, often drawing on their own experiences. Then the catechist shows the children the material and how to use this instrument that allows the child to continue the meditation during the long working time that is part of each catechetical session. This is the time that allows Christ to be the one Teacher (John Paul II, #6).

Gianna, in a paper presented in Torreon, Mexico, in September 1998, called these materials

> indications of the hidden reality of God. They are concrete helps to
> know the language, times, and places of the mystery of God. The child
> will make the mystery his own according to his own nature, his own
> capacities and his own personal rhythm of learning. With due respect
> for the differences, we can say that materials do what liturgy does.
> Our relationship with God is established through sensible objects,
> respecting a fundamental human exigency. (Gobbi)

The overall stance of the adult catechist is that in every presentation God speaks. There is no need for moralizing. The children, struck by the message, want to live in conformity with it, to be part of God's kingdom and share in its joy. In their own time they will incorporate just what it is that they need.

Facing Life and Death

An example of the child's ability to address his or her need is a presentation that is offered to children as young as three. It came about sometime in the 1980s as Sofia and Gianna worked with some young children confronted with the reality of death. They observed that even if a death is lived in a serene and peaceful way, there is still a question within the heart of the child: "What happens to the body?" "What is the destiny of the human body?" This question seems to be the crux of their encounter with death, the problem that is really their own. In a Chicago-area atrium, four-year-old Francis, after the death of his mother, silently drew pictures of gravestones in a cemetery at each atrium session.

The presentation known as The Mystery of Life and Death offers a way to answer the child's unspoken question by going to the words of Jesus in John 12:24: "Unless a grain of wheat falls into the earth and dies, it remains just a single grain; but if it dies, it bears much fruit." The material that helps the children experience these words consists of a tray holding plantings of wheat in three small pots, a glass box with wheat seeds, a scripture card that has a drawing of the stages of growth of the wheat with the verse from John, and a vase with stalks of wheat. Also available are some old newspapers.

The catechist recounts the planting of each seed: two weeks ago, one week ago, four days ago. The children examine first a seed from the box and then the three plants, all of them growing. They study together the drawing, then a stalk of wheat full of seeds. "One seed produces all these seeds. But it had to die. If the seed had stayed in the box and if it wasn't in the earth, all this growth wouldn't have taken place. In the earth it's all covered. It happens in the darkness."

Then the scripture card is introduced. "One time Jesus said: 'Unless a grain of wheat falls into the earth. . . .' " The children continue to meditate with the catechist. "The seed had to die. It had to go underneath. What do you see now? Another form, even more beautiful but completely different. It really makes you think: "Which do you think is richer, the seed or the wheat?" As the meditation progresses, the catechist may include a simple proclamation, such as, "When Jesus died and rose, he had a stronger life." There is the opportunity to prolong the meditation by overturning one or more of the plantings onto the newspapers to see what might be left of the seed.

This illustrates so well the objective and peripheral approach to catechesis that is the hallmark of Catechesis of the Good Shepherd. Aside from proclaiming the Resurrection, the death of a person is not spoken of in a direct or explicit way. The example of the seed is used for its own sake. Later, the children can recall it and make the connection to persons according to their need. It shows a profound respect for the delicacy of the child's inner life, which is an area where we cannot trespass. Often when we want to help we can easily intrude. Here we are offering reality and, to children who themselves are sick, much needed contact with the natural world. The doctrinal content of the presentation could be expressed in words found in a preface for funeral Masses: "Lord, for your faithful people life is changed, not ended."

Living with Christ

At the heart of this mode of catechesis is a biblical text that is fundamental to the life of a Christian. It is the parable-allegory of the Good Shepherd (John 10), the text used to introduce children to the person of Christ. This text poses a deep question: "Who are you, Jesus?" This is a prevailing question in the hearts of children even after they meet Jesus as the Good Shepherd. They ask not out of confusion or uncertainty, but because they know him and want to draw closer. It is an important question in the history of the Church. Indeed, councils were convened over it. But with children it is different. It is not about Jesus' nature, but rather, "Who are *you*, Lord?"

The child's focus seems to be the love of the Good Shepherd for each sheep, each one. This personal love, and the relationship built on it, is seen in a very common picture children draw in the atrium showing the Good Shepherd with words coming from his mouth that are the names of children. The part of John 10:3 that reads, "He calls his own sheep by name," is striking to the child. There are other important realities in the parable, of course—community (the flock), covenant (the sheep follow him), evil (the wolf), and an eschatological vision of abundant life with one flock and one shepherd. But relationship is the theme that seems to satisfy the spiritual hunger of children and will become the foundation of the moral life (Cavalletti, 1999, 13).

The parable holds a clear statement of who this shepherd is and the primary identifying event that characterizes him: "I am the good shepherd. The good shepherd lays down his life for the sheep" (John 10:11). What is held up for the children is a deeper and broader meaning than to lay down one's life by dying. Jesus puts his sheep first, gives them his love, his care, his attention, his whole self. Jesus offers a vital relationship—complete, inseparable, and intimate. "I know my own and my own know me" (John 10:14). These words describe the "definitive aim of catechesis," which the *General Directory of Catechesis* describes as "to put people not only in touch, but also in communion and intimacy, with Jesus Christ" (#80).

According to the ritual of an atrium presentation, the catechist first introduces the parable, letting the children know that Jesus once said, "I am the good shepherd," and leading them to wonder about these words. There is the solemn reading of the passage with lit candle, and then slowly the material is shown. "This is the sheepfold. This is the Good Shepherd. These are the sheep." With the small wood sheep in the sheepfold and the Good Shepherd facing them from the outside, the adult reads, "The Good Shepherd calls his own sheep by name and leads them out." Then in silence the sheep are slowly moved, one by one, out of the sheepfold, closer to the shepherd. Then the catechist reads verse four ("he goes ahead of them . . . the sheep follow") and the shepherd moves forward. One by one the sheep follow. The rest of the parable is read again as the children sit, enjoying the sight of ten sheep behind their shepherd. Later, when children work with this material, they show more than with any other work what it means to pray with a material (Cavalletti, 1992, 67–74).

For older children, the tandem parable of the True Vine is given: "I am the vine, you are the branches" (John 15:5). We are not only close to Jesus, we are part of him. The invitation to "abide" (John 15:4) is also an unspoken announcement. To abide in Christ we must already be in Christ (Cavalletti, 1996, 85).

The Response

It was to be expected that if the Catechesis of the Good Shepherd should ever be well received, it would certainly generate some criticism. It is an approach that is as different as it could be from both the standard series of textbooks and the lectionary-based liturgies with children. The criticism that has been openly stated seems to center around two facts: 1) it is too difficult to do, and 2) its proponents are unwilling to do anything else. Both statements are actually quite true. The Catechesis of the Good Shepherd makes great demands in terms of discipline, work, and initiative. It seems to border on foolishness to expect a volunteer parish catechist to be willing to take (and often even pay for) the 90-hour formation course in order to work with three- to six-year-olds. And once catechists are trained, they are openly committed to their very core and usually unwilling to turn back to a former way of catechizing children. Parishes often find that the request for a dedicated room as an atrium is the most difficult to fulfill.

What has actually happened in the United States is the primary response that can be given to the current criticism. Beginning in the late 1970s and into the 1980s, 20 to 25 catechists would come each summer for the one course that was offered. They often found themselves to be the only participant from their city. For eight summers Sofia herself came to give Level I and Level II courses, assisted by some of her American students, usually those who had trained with her in Rome. After the first Level III course in the summers of 1989 to 1990, trainings began to multiply—a few each year until the present offering of over 80 courses. Atria began to appear in isolated churches and schools with some dioceses having clusters of 20 to 30 sites. It became a "common ground" phenomenon attracting all persuasions of Catholics. In 1985 a few Episcopalians were drawn to the courses and now Episcopal churches have approximately half of the U.S. atria. There are also a few in United Methodist, Lutheran, and other Christian churches. This reception is truly mysterious, given the valid critique, but here are a few possible explanations.

1) *The ambitious nature of this Catechesis is very attractive.* Catechists do not want to be asked to do something too little or too trivial. They want to proclaim that which they know with their whole being is Good News. *Evangelii Nuntiandi* speaks of the "hidden energy" of the Good News (Paul VI, #4). The long, rich, retreat-like formation in which the adults receive the presentations before they are ever asked to give them has turned out to be one of the greatest assets of the Catechesis of the Good Shepherd.

2) *Though developing the atrium is a big task, it is not hurried or stressful work.* The slow pace of the formation seems to influence the pace with which an atrium is established in a parish. Once in a training course, catechists often feel they have found a lifelong ministry, therefore, why rush? They begin to meet with parents, make some materials, and elicit the help of other parishioners who have skills in woodworking, painting, sewing, sculpting. It quickly becomes apparent that it is not necessary to have an ideal atrium in the first year. The children are coming with longing and gratitude to the simplest atrium that has only a few presentations for each liturgical season. Jack, age four, climbed on top of his sleeping father at five in the morning: "Wake up, Dad. Today's the atrium."

3) *Parents confirmed what catechists were seeing in the child.* In the early days, when there were fewer than 20 atria in the country, catechists beginning the Catechesis of the Good Shepherd wondered how they would educate parents about an approach so different from the CCD classes of their generation. But in many instances parents turned out to be the ones who were knowledgeable. They sensed their children's hunger for God and desire to enjoy God. Parents know that today, more than ever before, children need the time and opportunity to wonder, to behold and marvel at something. Rather than lots of information or stimuli, they want something to dwell on—a mustard seed, yeast in flour, wine and water, the light of the paschal candle spreading to individual candles. Children need to know reality and they hunger for hope.

A key factor in gaining the favor of parents is that children want to come to the atrium. The older children are usually less outwardly enthusiastic than the younger ones, but they know they have found something wonderful there. Patricia Coulter, in *The Good Shepherd and the Child, A Joyful Journey,* writes, "When we reflect together with children, it helps them learn how to meditate by themselves" (Cavalletti, et al., 47).

One parent, who was not involved in the work of the atrium, nevertheless wrote in a parish publication about its intangible benefits:

> It is deceptively simple: these students of God go to a room filled with materials of Jesus' life and use these materials to teach themselves. Catholic rituals are named, explained and acted out so the children can be involved and pray on a deeper level with the church community.
>
> But the children must motivate themselves and use prayer as their helper. They may feel alone, confused or disinterested in their search, just as they will feel alone, confused or disinterested many times in their lives. But amidst this they will become familiar with God's love and are comforted by his presence. They learn how to pray both themselves and through the church to gain strength and understanding of all the challenges that will be placed in their paths.
>
> This does not come easily and religion class may be more fun if they watched movies or played games. But religion is not entertainment. Children need spiritual development that is much more permanent than that. Atrium provides them a sanctuary where *"they learn and grow through God's love."*
>
> Despite the clutter the world offers them, it is a sanctuary they will carry throughout their lives. (Brenda Scharping)

4) *The Catechesis of the Good Shepherd evangelizes adults.* Many young parents and catechists grew up in a transitional time for religious education, following Vatican II. Through involvement in this catechesis some of them are discovering the tradition for the first time. This discovery is true evangelization in that "the name, the teaching, the life, the promises, the kingdom, and the mystery of Jesus of Nazareth, the Son of God" are proclaimed to them (Paul VI #22).

5) *Concentric circles of support exist.* The Catechesis of the Good Shepherd operates in a very grassroots way. At the same time, it has a global presence, existing in various social settings in at least 20 countries. The Church, in all its diversity and in its many branches, has been fertile ground for this growth. In the United States, three graduate schools of ministry have offered its Level I course for credit. The largest publisher of parish resources has publications under a Catechesis of the Good Shepherd

imprint. Both Roman Catholic and Episcopal dioceses have organized and sponsored its formation courses for catechists.

This response suggests that the theological underpinnings of the work must be both obvious and strong. One sees immediately that it is grounded in the great dignity of the human person (even the smallest) in his or her relationship with God. The environment that is prepared for the child declares that God, unknowable and transcendent, can be reached through signs.

Conclusion

There are many speculations and no one knows for sure why the Catechesis of the Good Shepherd has grown the way it has. It may have to do with the gentle stewardship of a group of wise women catechists who form its international council. Or it may simply be that Sofia and Gianna have shown us how to allow catechesis to evolve at the bidding of children. They are women who know how to sleep, as it were, leaving the outcome to the Grower.

References

Catechesis of the Good Shepherd. 2000 *Journal* 15. Chicago: Liturgy Training Publications, 2000.

Cavalletti, Sofia. "Discovering the Real Spiritual Child (Part 1)." The *NAMTA Journal,* 24.2 (1999) 7–16. (Available videotaped address from Liturgy Training Publications under the title "Discovering the Real Spiritual Life of Children").

———. *Il potenziale religioso tra 6 e i 12 anni.* Rome: Citta Nuova, 1996.

———. *The Religious Potential of the Child,* trans. Patricia M. Coulter and Julie M. Coulter. Chicago: Liturgy Training Publications, 1992.

Cavalletti, Sofia, et al. *The Good Shepherd and the Child: A Joyful Journey.* Chicago: Liturgy Training Publications, 1996.

General Directory for Catechesis. Washington, DC: United States Catholic Conference, 1998.

Gobbi, Gianna. "The Essence and Use of Materials." Unpublished paper presented at the Second Seminar for Formation Leaders. Torreon, Mexico, September 1998.

John Paul II. *Catechesi Tradendae* (On Catechesis in Our Time) Apostolic Exhortation, 1979.

John Paul VI. *Evangelii Nuntiandi* (On Evangelization in the Modern World), Apostolic Exhortation, 1975.

Scharping, Brenda. "Listening to the Gentle Message of God's Presence." Reflections of Faith, St. Catherine Parish, Milwaukee, WI.

This essay was first published as "The Catechesis of the Good Shepherd" in the August 2001 issue of New Theology Review. *Used with permission.*

Familiar Faces and Places

Via degli Orsini

Clock tower, as seen from Sofia's study

Above: Sofia and
a child

Left: Sofia working
with Structure of
the Mass chart

Above:
Sofia in
her study

Right:
Gianna Gobbi
Assisi, 1997

Top: Sofia, Tilde Cocchini, and daughters Francesca and Patrizia in Israel

Bottom: Tilde and Francesca Cocchini

© 2004 Suzanne Haraburd

Right:
Sofia, next to
model of the city
of Jerusalem

Below:
Sofia, Bishop
Frank T. Griswold,
Gianna Gobbi

© 2004 Elizabeth Piper

Top: Sofia, Gianna, and friends, 1997 International Council

Bottom: Flaminia Guidi, Patricia Stenton, Gianna

© 2004 Patricia Stenton

Above:
Maria Christlieb
with map of
the growth of
the Catachesis
in Mexico

Right:
Gianna in her
workshop

© 2004 Patricia Stenton

Above: Francesca
Cocchini with
9- to 12-year-old
children

Left: Rebekah
Rojcewicz, Maria
Ludlow

Top: Gianna, Silvana, Sofia, and Tilde

Bottom: Sofia and Linda Kaiel

A History of Growth in Joy

Lupita Palafox

July 2004 will mark 28 years since that first July of 1976 in Mexico City, when some 30 of us found ourselves opening our eyes and ears attentively, as we tried to assimilate the impact that the person and the words of Dr. Sofia Cavalletti, so full of faith and wisdom, were having on us. That event was the first Catechesis of the Good Shepherd course Sofia gave in Latin America.

Some of us already had considerable experience in catechetics, while others were just beginning in this field. Sofia invited both groups to go deeper, to discover an authentically biblical image of the God who loves us, and to live in a new way a real encounter with God, through the eyes and hearts of children.

Those of us who lived that first experience know that it marked our minds and our hearts definitively, not only for the purpose of sharing this deeper understanding with the children, but for our own personal and family lives as well.

Throughout the past 27 years, the powerful seed planted during Sofia's initial visit has been germinating. Above all, this growth has occurred thanks to the Lord, our Good Shepherd, who from the beginning awakened in most of us—over 90 percent— a true vocation to dedicate a significant part of our lives to this catechesis. We felt driven to help our own children live a real encounter with God and thereby assist in the integral formation of their lives.

In Mexico, after that first course in 1976, we had the good fortune, the gift of the Lord, to receive Sofia again, sometimes alone and other times with some of her worthy collaborators, Gianna Gobbi, Silvana Montanaro, Tilde Cocchini, and Francesca Cocchini. For four more summers—from 1979 to 1982—they shared with us their experience and profound theological, liturgical, and pedagogical background in intensive courses.

The translation and printing of Sofia's and Gianna's books were initiated very early in Mexico, thanks to the Lord and to generous people who supported us in this aspect of the work. Beginning in 1980, some Mexican catechists were able to start going to Rome for prolonged periods in order to continue our formation with Sofia and Gianna. From then on we began, little by little, to offer formation to other Mexican catechists and thus share the riches that we had been able to absorb in Rome.

After the Catechesis of the Good Shepherd took root in Mexico City and Chihuahua, this catechesis was in great demand and spread throughout the Republic of Mexico—in Merida, Morelia, Juarez, Torreon, Guadalajara—always through the initiative of those women and others who themselves had heard about or lived some of the experiences of this catechesis and asked us to help them with formation. We have never had to do any kind of advertisement for the courses. On the contrary, at times we had to ask catechists to wait, because there were not always formation leaders available to give courses.

In the early years, following the first course in Mexico with Sofia, we catechists began our work and formation in various atria, in different places and social settings in Mexico City and Chihuahua City. The majority of the atria were attached to parishes, but others were in schools. From these initial atria, many other people became interested in working in this catechesis. As had happened in Rome, the spread of this work was driven by the joy of the children and of the catechists.

Currently this work has extended to 17 states in Mexico. For us, the Catechesis of the Good Shepherd had been something that, even though we didn't know it clearly, we had been waiting for and needing for our children, and also for ourselves. What answered our unexpressed need was, on the one hand, the content: the "announcement" or message of the God who is transcendent and yet totally near; God, the source of love, who is so near as to communicate His very life in order to bring us to believe; the God of history who builds with us, through history, a "plan of communion." And on the other hand, the experience of a real encounter with God, in the catechesis itself, answered a deep, unspoken desire; this real encounter occurs as we listen to the Word, meditate on it, and deeply enjoy it, because in it God communicates to us His plan—God's will to form a covenant with humanity. This catechesis has awakened in us a response, formed not only of words of admiration and praise, but of life. All this richness has fulfilled and greatly surpassed our expectations. After 27 years of continuous work with the children, we catechists remain enthusiastic, in spite of the obstacles that are found in trying to follow the ways of the Lord, and in spite of our own limitations. We realize fully what our work is: principally the work of the Lord.

Some bishops and priests in Mexico have supported us, convinced of the value and richness of this catechesis. Others respect us and let us work. We have many examples of those clergy who are open to learning and going deeper into this catechesis, because they have seen the enormous capacity of the child to receive and enjoy the message—that "religious potential" pointed out and admired by Sofia. These bishops and priests have been a great support, or rather I could say they have valued our work in the pastoral action of the Church.

I want to mention the first bishops who offered us their full support: Bishop Francisco Maria Aguilera, who in 1976 was president of the Commission for Evangelization and Catechesis on the national level, and Bishop Adalberto Almeida of Chihuahua, now both emeritus.

Bishop Aguilera learned of Sofia's work before 1976, while he was in Rome, and according to his words, the Catechesis of the Good Shepherd "represents one of the most noteworthy advances in catechetics," in which "there breathes a sacred respect for the child, for the child's mysterious capacity of essentiality and contemplation, of sincerity and openness with God and with others."

Bishop Almeida opened his diocese to the Catechesis of the Good Shepherd and facilitated the formation of a team of catechists, thus enabling this catechesis to be established in nearly all the parishes of that diocese. Still today, thousands of children, together with hundreds of catechists, receive and live the message there.

Permit me to quote a few lines from records we have kept through the years, which seem to me to best express how the Catechesis of the Good Shepherd has been received by the children of Mexico:

> The announcement of the Word of God fills the children with joy, and this joy becomes evident in an improvement of their physical well-being. (From the Association for Aid to Cerebral Palsy [APAC] after the children had experienced the Catechesis of the Good Shepherd)

> . . . The experience was one of great love, joy, and tranquillity in the lives of both children and adults (parents and catechist). (From an agency that cares for a group of mentally retarded children in Mexico City)

The children surround the catechist and beg her: "We want to go to the atrium every day! When is it Wednesday?"(From a school where atrium sessions are held once a week)

In working with some of the children, youth, and adults from rural areas, we have seen that certain presentations in Catechesis of the Good Shepherd, like the History of the Reign of God, hold a particular significance for them. They reveal to them a sense of their personal dignity, showing them, for example, the value and greatness of the work of their own hands in the building of the reign of God. (From a catechist)

For these children also [the catechesis] is a source of joy, peace, and *"innamoramento."* . . . little by little the relationships within the families are being transformed; it is bringing them the discovery of the great dignity of the child. (From a catechist working in marginalized squatter communities)

The children participate freely; they laugh and show great happiness. After the meditation on the True Vine in the preparation for his first Communion, one little boy touched one of the branches, and though unable to see it, he exclaimed spontaneously, "It's so beautiful, so very green!" (From a catechist who works in the cities of Chihuahua and Guadalajara where the catechists have worked with children and teenagers who are blind, translating part of the material into braille, and using distinctive textures to represent the different liturgical colors)

It is not easy to proclaim a Good Shepherd full of love to children who lack, almost totally, the experience of feeling themselves loved. . . . It has been a most beautiful though difficult experience. . . . The reward has been in seeing the peace and joy of these other "little ones" of the kingdom who so need to know and feel loved and valued for their own sake. (From a catechist in Guadalajara)

The children listen amazed and meditate with joy on the Word which comes forth from the mouth of God, who gives them his love, even in their difficult state of life. (From a catechist who works with orphaned children)

The fruits on these branches of the Vine are beautiful and special:
Moments of conversion, of drawing nearer to God, and of deepening
in the faith are being lived in the family each Saturday afternoon
in those who listen, meditate, and celebrate the Word. There is now
in these families a common language of prayer. The Catechesis is
becoming faith and life. (From a catechist in the city of Torreon)

For the last three years that loving presence of God has been announced
to a group of children of parents who are inmates of a prison. The
Lord is helping them to feel trust and has given them his peace. (From
a catechist)

In varied environments, within different socioeconomic realities,
among families who face many different obstacles and challenges, the atti-
tudes of the children are moving their parents and caregivers to make it possible for them to go to the atrium. In many groups, the mothers who are
catechists feel conscientiously committed to continue because of the results
they see in the children, who have formed a relationship, not with a God
who guides them by rules and fear, but "with the Lord, God of life and history," who fills all their moments with the divine presence, including the
times they don't feel understood or valued, as well as those moments when
the feelings of being loved by parents, teachers, and friends are a reflection
of the love and nearness of God.

All of this beautiful work, we firmly believe, has been accomplished
thanks to the Lord, our Good Shepherd, who has allowed us to put our
small effort together with His strong and loving action. How can we ever
thank Him enough!

Translated by Kathy Dahl-Bredine

A Transforming Moment: Kingdom Song

Ignatius Feaver, OFM CAP

Some of the following memories were shared with fellow catechists on the occasion of the 25th anniversary of the Catechesis of the Good Shepherd in Canada, celebrated in 2003.

In the summer of 1978, I went to Houston, Texas, to take a course in early childhood catechesis. This month-long formation experience was in the Catechesis of the Good Shepherd, a method completely unfamiliar to me, and was offered by Sofia Cavalletti, someone I'd never heard of before. My experience during that month is a wonderful example of how grace surprises and moves us; what happened in that course transformed my spiritual life. That month in Houston was like being held by God and gently introduced to the mysteries of delight and wonder, as Sofia "opened" the Catechesis of the Good Shepherd both in her lectures and in presenting the "work" of the atrium. The purpose of the course was to demonstrate to us how to present the catechetical materials to the child; yet something very deep within me was profoundly touched, and the child within me burst forth. The very focus of this work, to help the child "fall in love with God," happened in me!

During the course, I was deeply moved when Sofia presented the *Fettuccia,* a material that illustrates the vastness of the history of the kingdom. For perhaps the first time, I felt that as a unique child of God my presence in this long history of salvation was not insignificant.

Sofia invited the course participants to present one of the catechetical materials to the group. Another participant and I chose to present together the *Fettuccia.* In the long cloister walk of St. Thomas Seminary, we unfolded the history of salvation as we meditatively and contemplatively walked this incredible story of God's love. After the presentation there was a long moment of quiet. People were deeply struck by the material; later, they slowly drifted to places where they could be alone to ponder and savor this experience.

In my own solitude, I found myself with guitar in hand; then some notes and words found their way into a song. What emerged was a "Song of the Kingdom." I was surprised and filled with wonder! I had never written a song before, nor even had a desire to do so. Yet, from some deep place within me came . . . words and music.

Later I sang this song as the Communion meditation at our Eucharist during the course. The other participants were amazed because the words and the music connected with their own experience of having walked the history of the kingdom.

A couple of years later I was in Rome and visited Sofia. She was accompanying the children on the first Communion retreat. She asked if I would sing this "Song of the Kingdom" for the children. After a moment of hesitation, I began to sing, summoning up something of the same childlike trust as the children who sat around me to listen to the song. I sang in English. They only spoke Italian. Yet, they understood! Like in Houston, there was silence . . . something mysterious was touched in us. Then a little boy, with a sense of awe in this voice said, *"Bellissimo!"* I do not necessarily have a good voice nor do I play the guitar well. What was "beautiful" for this little one was our common experience of the loving embrace of our God in the story of salvation!

During my most recent visit to Rome, I journeyed one evening to visit with Sofia. We spent an hour and a half in conversation, and as we spoke, once again I heard her say that we must never stop listening to what is essential for the children; they are our teachers. She told me that she sensed it is the child who will teach us how to pray, for prayer, which is "holy conversation," is essentially simple. Recalling that Jesus said, "Let the little children come to me" (Matthew 19:14), Sofia observed that the littleness of the child invites us into the "littleness" of our God, which is the same "littleness" that we see in the sacred bread of the Eucharist, in the manger, and in the brokenness of the cross. I left Sofia's feeling full with a fullness of God's Spirit as though a gesture of epiclesis had been made over me. *Bellissimo!*

Modern Montessori in Search of a Soul

David Kahn

> Help us, O God, to enter into the secret of childhood so that we may
> know, love, and serve the child in accordance with the laws of thy
> justice and following thy holy will.
>
> Maria Montessori, *The Absorbent Mind*

> The child is the essence of spirituality.
>
> Mario Montessori, "Dr. Maria Montessori and the Child"

Sofia Cavalletti's and Gianna Gobbi's catechesis, in its magnitude, stands alone as a great work, even apart from the Montessori tradition. The implications of its Judeo-Christian framework are well appreciated by those who continue their work. As the Montessori movement has come into the spotlight in the field of alternative education, it has suppressed, if not eliminated, its Christian connections, especially in the United States, where a non-sectarian model is in demand. This secularization of Montessori allows for spiritual expression, but not that of a specific religious tradition. As the religious core of Montessori practice slowly disappears, both in Montessori pedagogy and in the home, there is an increasing void left by the lack of religious roots and principles, which have traditionally responded to the child's true spiritual needs.

Sofia Cavalletti and Gianna Gobbi have had the wisdom to see the spiritual potential of the child rooted in a specific religious practice. Dr. Cavalletti stated her unconditional belief in the benefit of a specific religious tradition during a teleconference from Rome for a gathering of the North American Montessori Teachers' Association in Fort Worth, Texas, in 1999:

> To be faithful to my tradition—is it a limitation? In some sense it is,
> but I have to remember here that there is another basic human need:
> the need to belong. We want to belong to a family, to a country, to

a culture, and so on. To be a citizen of the world is a very noble ideal and aspiration, but there is a risk in it: the risk of becoming somebody without roots, somebody who has no soil under his or her feet.

In this regard, we have to learn a lesson from nature; in nature there are many trees, small ones and big ones, and in order to be alive they have to strictly observe a rule: the breadth of the foliage has to correspond to the size of the roots. If there is not a balance between the foliage and the roots, the tree will fall down and die.

In the human being, the roots are our traditions and the foliage is the capacity to be open to wider and wider horizons. We have to take care of both. Only if we are firmly bound to our soil—our tradition—will we be able to have a vital interchange with other cultures and traditions. Only if we are firmly rooted in our tradition will we be able to offer others our richness, be open to receive others' richness, and be capable of taking advantage of it.

If the balance between fidelity to one's tradition and open-mindedness to other visions of the world is not reached, we risk becoming sterile and losing our personality. ("Discovering the Real Spiritual Child," 15)

The essential practice of a faith as a "living out" of spirituality through a system of symbols and signs, a repeating liturgical year, a clear source of moral guidance, a tradition of worship, a specific theology attached to worship, and a scriptural understanding of the Old and New Testaments is the approach strongly conveyed by Sofia Cavalletti, as it was first articulated by Maria Montessori in her book *The Child in the Church:*

> But if the adult needs not only to know but to "live" his religion, the need is all the greater for the child—who is more adapted to live it than to know it. Are not the limits of the problem concerning the religious education of the child identical with those of the various methods of learning and memorizing? In fact, knowledge in our case is nothing else but the first indispensable step in opening the paths of life to the child.

So Montessori and her priest collaborators proceeded to link her seminal ideas of the prepared environment to the Church:

The result was the opening of "The Children's House in the Church," founded by Father Casulleras, and a new life began there—that of "The Little Ones Living in the Church." At the same time, the Montessori Method was furnished with a long-sought opportunity of penetrating deeper into the life of the child's soul, and of thus fulfilling its true educational mission.

The first step was "to prepare the place" for the *bambini* (*The Child in the Church*, 23).

Montessori saw the concept of an atrium, a special room for prayer, as the final application of what the children learned in the classroom:

> One could see how little children, because of their innocence, can feel the need of God's presence in a purer and more intense manner, even if less definitely than adults. Their souls seem to be more open to divine intuitions than those of adults, despite their less perfectly developed intelligence and skill in reasoning.
>
> Meanwhile, the application of the method followed in my "Children's Houses" produced this excellent fruit—the Church almost seemed to be the end of the education which the method proposed to give. The "silence" observed in class, to accustom the child to recollection, here found its application. It became the interior recollection observed in the House of God, amid the gentle flickering of the candlelight in an atmosphere dim, yet resplendent with gleaming white and gold. Again their actions were practically repetitions of what they had learned to do in the classroom; walking silently, placing chairs quietly, standing up and sitting down gracefully and passing between benches and bystanders without knocking against them. (*The Child in the Church*, 23–24)

The initial conception that the child has a unique relationship with God, which can be supported by a specific prepared environment within the Children's House, is the framework that Cavalletti and Gobbi inherited from the Montessori legacy. Dr. Cavalletti sees the catechists' work as an immense research ("The Spiritual Development of the Child," 12) around the world within all different cultural and economic backgrounds. The adult observes the spontaneous responses of children as they, *by themselves,* encounter God within a prepared environment. *"Help me to do it by myself."*

Cavalletti speaks of a new child: "I dare say that I have seen a *metaphysical child* in the true sense of the word. . . . I have seen a child capable of seeing the invisible" ("Spiritual Development," 13).

Anecdotal evidence from children in their various forms of expression, their extraordinary capacity for prayer, and the child's search for what is essential reveal to catechists that God and the child have a unique relationship, particularly before the age of six. The Montessori principles require that the adult step aside and help the children to help themselves. In the context of religious formation, the adult assists with God's work, but the spirit of God within the child directs the work. The adult's role in relation to the prepared environment is elevated to a new status in a religious context. The signs and symbols, the scripture and liturgy, the presentation of the parables are all part of the prepared environment, which leads the child to God. A new paradigm is clarified for all Montessorians, catechists or not, which is to observe the *divine mystery* of the child's natural and spontaneous activities.

When Montessori linked her educational method to a specific faith, Catholicism, she sought the real meaning of what is meant by "catholic" or universal. An example of the universal is the parable of the Good Shepherd. Jesus is the Good Shepherd, who knows each of his sheep by name, who defends them against wild animals, and who searches for the lost sheep, thereby giving the children feelings of security and belonging. God is there not as judge, but as protector. God reveals himself as love. The search for God is a real journey for the three- to six-year-old, and it is this reality of nurture that supports all the areas of the child's work, for the Protector is always present. The non-religious prepared environment also protects the child under six by creating a place where he or she encounters the work of self-formation: "our schools offer the tinies a sheltering refuge in which the first elements of character can take shape, each of which has its own importance" (Montessori, *The Absorbent Mind*, 275).

Likewise, Montessori describes the Children's House as providing "the spirit of the family or the tribe" (*The Absorbent Mind*, 288). If the child believes that the Good Shepherd is Jesus and that she is a member of his flock, this feeling easily transfers to the parents, the family, the Montessori guide, and the social life of the children in the Children's House environment. The application is universal and not specific to Catholic liturgy and doctrine.

If Montessori catechesis is part of the historical foundation of the work of the Children's House, it also provides a substantial dimension to

Cosmic Education for children ages six to twelve. In the opening chapter of her book *Living Liturgy,* Dr. Cavalletti establishes parameters connecting creation with Cosmic Education:

> The range of God's plan is cosmic, embracing all things that are in heaven and on earth (Ephesians 1:10). And "every creature in heaven and on earth and under the earth and in the sea, and all that is in them" is called to participate in the universal praise of God (Revelation 5:13). In this all-encompassing framework of time and space, what is liturgy's function during the period of history in which we are living?
>
> In order to understand this point, it might be helpful to pause a moment and ponder the work of creation of the world. Let's imagine we were witness to this: We saw the formless world being born, and then we saw it gradually take shape and become organized. We saw vegetable and animal life begin. With admiration we contemplated the world as it grew continually more beautiful, and, moved by wonder, we asked ourselves, "Why? What is the purpose of all this?" (*Living Liturgy,* 7)

In the context of the Catechesis of the Good Shepherd, the creation story is experienced as an article of faith; the mystery of creation and creator is considered a fundamental and universal truth. These convictions of faith add fervor to a secular vision of the birth of the universe, of the coming of life on earth, of the evolving human from *Australopithecus* to *Homo sapiens.*

It is a teacher's enthusiasm for belief in the cosmic purpose of life that has a personal impact on the moral and emotional well-being of an elementary child. But if Cavalletti's integration of God and creation brings the religious dimension of purpose and identity into the epic of life on earth, the child who experiences these realities will have the background to penetrate the meaning of the *God Who Has No Hands* (a religious "cosmic tale" that is the opening "Great Lesson" of the Montessori elementary program) in a different way. The child who has a relationship with God will incorporate the implicit religious content of this Great Lesson into his personal belief system, which already is open to a cosmic message:

> In the worship of God, we bring our whole lives with us, even that activity in which we use and enjoy the goods of this world. In worship, we also bring elements of the lower scale of nature with us that are

transformed by the work of our hands and mind. In worship, the human creature . . . consecrates the whole universe to God. The action that worship enacts is cosmic. (Cavalletti, *Living Liturgy* 10)

The nonsectarian approach to spirituality—one that speaks of awe and wonder, of openness to creative forces of the universe, of contemplation of the great questions of the universe, of a sacred connection to all of life, and of a oneness with the universe (Wolf, 10), can indeed communicate a greater good. Montessori suggested that religion has a unique role when presenting Cosmic Education:

What is most wanted is no patronizing charity for humanity, but
a reverent consciousness of its dignity and worth. This should be cultivated in the same way as a religious sentiment, which indeed should
be in us all, for we should not need to be reminded that no man can love
God while remaining indifferent to his neighbour. (*To Educate the
Human Potential*, 18)

When Montessori speaks of integrating religion and cosmic science, she is very straightforward:

Truly it is no new idea . . . for children first to be taught the creation
of the world and man's place in it, . . . in the light of religion and
philosophy. The answer was ever what it still is, "God has set you upon
the earth to work and do your duty!" This principle can now, however,
be developed on a scientific plan, and be made far more attractive.
(*To Educate the Human Potential*, 7)

In 1984, the Association for the Catechesis of the Good Shepherd was established, with its main aim to involve adults and children in a common religious experience in which the religious values of childhood are predomi- nant. Montessori philosophy is based in the revelation of the love principle; Montessori's version of evolution places biological process in the hands of God, with a "final cause" to which evolution gravitates with an ever- emerging human vision. The nonsectarian spiritual position can convey this vision in Montessori, but it cannot stand alone without the rejuvenation of a "living faith" that can provide an alternative to modern uncertainty. So the Montessori movement depends on a faith tradition not only to augment

Cosmic Education, but to hold in place a value system of unselfishness in service and worship beyond the Montessori prepared environment.

The Montessori movement must explore its religious roots, for unless we link our spiritual traditions with our wider horizons we will float into oblivion; we will be limited in what we can offer as unique, personal, and distinctly sensitive to the metaphysical child.

Montessori wrote in 1952, on the eve of her death, a letter to the Catholic Montessori Guild teachers' meeting in London:

> Take then, as help in your tasks, with faith and humility, "the all-powerful children" (Benedict XV). Take as your special task to watch that their limpid light not be dimmed. Protect in their development those natural energies implanted in the souls of children by the guiding hand of God. (Untitled message, 1)

Sofia Cavalletti is a champion of the soul of humanity. I have met her several times, and in her loving, gentle manner she embodied the humility and sacredness of her revelations of the metaphysical child. If she had not been a contributor, the Montessori community today could not even imagine "education to wonder and the Kingdom of God" (*The Religious Potential of the Child,* 138). For Montessori's promised land lies somewhere between science and religion, beyond charted waters, deep in the soul of every child. Sofia Cavalletti still carries the beaming lamp that shows us the way in search of a spiritual place that is paradoxically attached to modern reality. Her famous passage has made a lasting impression:

> The nature of wonder is not a force that pushes us passively from behind; it is situated ahead of us and attracts us with irresistible force toward the object of our astonishment; it makes us advance toward it, filled with enchantment.
>
> Wonder is a dynamic value; nevertheless it does not drive us to activism but draws us to activity, to an activity we do as persons immersed in the contemplation of something that exceeds us. Maybe the particularity of wonder is that we find activity and contemplation inseparably blended within it.
>
> I would like to elucidate right away that in speaking about wonder I do not intend to talk about something like Alice in Wonderland. Wonder is a very serious thing that, rather than leading us away from

reality, can arise only from an attentive education that helps us to go always more deeply into reality. If we skim over things, we will never be surprised by them. Wonder is not an emotion of superficial people; it strikes root only in the person whose mind is able to settle and rest in things, in the person who is capable of stopping and looking. It is only through a continued and profound observation of reality that we become conscious of its many aspects, of the secrets and mysteries it contains. Openness to reality and openness to wonder proceed at the same pace; as we gradually enter into what is real, our eyes will come to see it as more and more charged with marvels, and wonder will become a habit of our spirit. . . .

Wonder is proper to the child, poet, artist, and also to the old person who has known how to live by beholding and contemplating the world surrounding him in such a way that reality has revealed ever widening horizons to him. (*The Religious Potential of the Child,* 138–39)

Amen. So be it! Thank you.

References

Cavalletti, Sofia. "Discovering the Real Spiritual Child (Part 1)." The *NAMTA Journal,* 24.2 (1999, Spring), 7–16.

———. *Living Liturgy: Elementary Reflections.* Chicago: Liturgy Training Publications, 1998.

———. *The Religious Potential of the Child: Experiencing Scripture and Liturgy with Young Children.* New York: Paulist Press, 1983.

———. "The Spiritual Development of the Child." *Montessori Talks to Parents,* 1.3 (1979), 12–14.

Montessori, Maria. *The Absorbent Mind.* 1949. Madras, India: Kalakshetra, 1992.

———. *The Child in the Church.* 1929. St. Paul: Catechetical Guild, 1965.

———. *To Educate the Human Potential.* 1948. Oxford: Clio, 1989.

———. Untitled message to Catholic teachers in London. *The Catechesis of the Good Shepherd,* 10 (1994, Spring), 1.

Montessori, Mario. "Dr. Maria Montessori and the Child." In *The Spiritual Hunger of the Modern Child: A Series of Ten Lectures.* Charles Town, WV: Claymont Communications, 1984 (43–65).

Wolf, Aline D. *Nurturing the Spirit in Non-Sectarian Classrooms.* Altoona, PA: Parent Child Press, 1996.

The Secure Child: Attachment and Emotional Development in the Atrium

Barbara Schmich Searle

One year after Maria Montessori opened the first Children's House in Rome, Italy, John Bowlby was born in London, England. In 1952, the year of Montessori's death, Bowlby, also a psychiatrist, published his first major work, a report for the World Health Organization, titled *Child Care and the Growth of Love*. It is unlikely that these two people ever met each other, and yet they shared a profound kinship in their love for the child and in their desire for each child's optimal development. Since Montessori's philosophy and approach are well known to the readers of this volume, this paper will concentrate on the work of Bowlby, and those researchers after him who elaborated on his basic insights. It will also attempt to integrate their findings into the three to six atrium setting, and assist the catechist in observing, describing, and assisting each individual child's growth toward security.

Attachment Theory

John Bowlby's attachment theory (Bowlby 1969/1982, 1973, 1980) postulates a biological and social behavioral system inherent in the infant and designed to maintain proximity to the mother or primary caretaker. The mother figure provides the infant with 1) a safe haven to which the infant can return in times of distress and 2) a secure base from which the infant can explore the environment. Bowlby draws upon systems control theory to explain the dynamics of attachment: distress provokes the child's need for the safe haven; when that need is met the infant has a secure base from which to venture forth; then the child engages in exploratory behavior, until such time as a new distress is felt and the attachment system is reactivated.

Attachments are directed toward specific individuals, are usually of long duration, and serve the function of survival. Although particularly evident in early childhood, "attachment behavior is held to characterize human beings from the cradle to the grave" (Bowlby, 1979, 129). It cannot be reduced to a childhood need for food or sexual needs in later development; it is something that can neither be outgrown nor deemed pathological.

The concept of the "working model," an important tenet of Bowlby's theory, explains how the child's experience of the primary caretaker's presence and availability (or lack of it) becomes internalized. Persistent interactional patterns become represented in the form of expectations about the caregiver and about the self (Holmes, 1993). A child develops a positive or negative view of the other as accessible or not, and a positive or negative view of the self as worthy of love or not. This working model is often generalized to other relationships, continuing to operate in circumstances beyond those which gave rise to it—in the form of assumptions and expectations about the self and others. It is, then, a kind of semipermanent template which influences future relationships, but which operates below the level of awareness.

It is Mary Ainsworth's empirical research (Ainsworth, 1967; Ainsworth & Wittig, 1969) with children in the Strange Situation that gives Bowlby's theory its most commonly used categories to label working models, *securely attached,* and two categories of insecurely attached, *anxious-ambivalent* and *avoidant.* Infants who are separated from their mother-figures respond in different ways when reunited: *Securely attached* infants, who generally receive consistent support, actively seek their mother-figure; *anxious-ambivalent* infants, who receive inconsistent parenting, show a combination of contact seeking and angry tantrums; *avoidant* infants, who receive insensitive and distant treatment, show little response to the return of the caregiver. Observations of children who do not fit well into any of these three categories have led some researchers to postulate a fourth, *disorganized/disoriented* (Main, Kaplan & Cassidy, 1985; Main & Solomon, 1986). These infants exhibit no clear strategy for dealing with the reunion of their caretaker, which appears to be due to the fact that there are deeply disturbing aspects to the caregiver's presence.

In speaking of working models it is tempting to think of them as purely cognitive schemas, but this would hardly be faithful to Bowlby's presentation. In his view, the emotional experience of a child actually precedes the formation of his or her working model. "During the earliest years of our lives, indeed, emotional expression and reception are the only means of communication we have, so that the foundations of our working models of self and attachment figure are perforce laid using information from that source alone" (Bowlby, 1988, 157). Throughout his writings he refers to attachment relationships as if they were a school of emotion:

> Many of the most intense emotions arise during the formation, the main-
> tenance, the disruption and the renewal of attachment relationships.
> The formation of a bond is described as falling in love, maintaining a
> bond as loving someone, and losing a partner as grieving over someone.
> Similarly, threat of loss arouses anxiety and actual loss gives rise to
> sorrow; whilst each of these situations is likely to arouse anger. The
> unchallenged maintenance of a bond is experienced as a source of secu-
> rity and the renewal of a bond as a source of joy. Because such emotions
> are usually a reflection of the state of a person's affectional bonds,
> the psychology and psychopathology of emotion is found to be in
> large part the psychology and psychopathology of affectional bonds.
> (Bowlby, 1979, 130)

If all goes well, the child and his or her attachment figure experience intense pleasure in their closeness and in their communication of affection. Between the pair there is much social interaction and the mother-figure is highly responsive to the baby's signals. Love and joy characterize the rela- tionship (Bowlby, 1969/1982). If all does not go well and there is a failure or interruption of the attachment bond, negative feelings will result. Bowlby and his colleagues observed the typical sequence when a child is separated from his or her attachment figure:

> At first he *protests* vigorously and tries by all the means available
> to him to recover his mother. Later he seems to *despair* of recovering
> her but nonetheless remains preoccupied with her and vigilant for
> her return. Later still he seems to lose his interest in his mother and to
> become emotionally *detached* from her.
>   After being reunited with his mother his attachment to her
> emerges afresh (but)whenever he suspects he will lose her again he
> exhibits acute *anxiety*. (Bowlby, 1973, 26–27)

Although this scenario focuses upon the impact of physical separation on the attachment bond, Bowlby is careful to include the possibility of a mother being physically present but emotionally absent. If the mother is unresponsive to her child's emotional needs because of her own impaired state, her own preoccupations, or a rigid approach to discipline, she is, from the point of view of relationship, unavailable to the child (Bowlby, 1973). Further examples of such unavailability can be found in "rejection, loss of love (perhaps on advent of a new baby or on account of mother's depression), alienation from one parent by the other . . . all [of which] have as a common factor loss by the child of a parent to love and attach himself to" (Bowlby, 1979, 64). It seems likely that children who are deprived of a loving attachment, whether it be through physical or psychological means, experience the same pattern of negative emotions: protest, anxiety, despair, and detachment.

If emotions are the foundation for secure and insecure attachments, it is likely that they will persist along with the working models the child constructs and influence subsequent emotional functioning. Secure attachment, involving a predominance of positive emotionality, can open a child to more experiences of positive emotion, whereas insecure attachment, involving a predominance of negative emotionality, can open a child to more experiences of negative emotion.

Neuropsychologists are theorizing about the biological effects of attachment patterns, suggesting that they become part of the chemistry of the brain and the operations of the nervous system (e.g., Kramer, 1992; Shore, 1994). Regardless of whether the author focuses on chemical explanations or the involvement of specific areas of the brain, they share common assumptions about brain development in infants: that a child is born with an overabundance of components of neural pathways and only those which are used are preserved; that the development of the brain is a dialectic process which requires social interaction provided by the environment; that attachment behavior does not merely overlay basic brain function nor contribute the "software" for existing pathways, but actually creates neurobiological structures.

Although Bowlby only hints at the possibility of a neurobiological substructure underlying attachment behavior (Bowlby, 1982), his own survey of contemporary research suggests that once a person has experienced insecure attachment emotions, these are more likely to reappear in other contexts. Insecure attachment is associated with differences in susceptibility to fear and the manifestations of phobias of various types (Bowlby, 1973), with pathological mourning (Bowlby, 1980) and with misdirected and inappropriate aggression (Bowlby, 1979). While anxious attachment is more associated with subsequent anxiety disorders, and avoidant attachment more associated with aggressivity, disordered mourning and depressive states in general seem to be associated with all forms of insecure attachment. Although it is an accepted feature of Bowlby's theory that "patterns established in parent–child relationships tend to structure the quality of later adult–adult relationships" (Bartholomew, 1993, 300), this reading of Bowlby suggests that the propensity to negative emotions generalizes even beyond the realm of relationship and finds new objects and outlets in the course of subsequent development. This is in line with Bowlby's approach to lability and stability of attachment organization: in the first two years attachment is the property of the dyad, but after that it becomes increasingly the property of the individual child (Bowlby, 1969/1982). The original emotions experienced vis-à-vis the mother figure could be thought of as not only being retained in the bodily memory of the child, adolescent, and adult, but actually shaping all subsequent emotional experience.

Emotional Development

It is understandable, then, that researchers from various theoretical perspectives would, after Bowlby, turn their attention to the emotional development of the infant and young child (e.g., Brown, 1993; Greenspan, 1997; Stern, 1985). The more that is understood by parents and caregivers about optimal emotional development, the more quickly deviations can be seen and healing interventions initiated. Greenspan's work is especially helpful in this regard because he has written not only for professional audiences but also for parents. With his wife, Nancy Thorndike Greenspan, he wrote *First Feelings: Milestones in the Emotional Development of Your Baby and Child* (Greenspan & Greenspan, 1985), which brought together contemporary research about how infants and young children progress through predictable emotional stages, and offered insights into how the emotional situation of the parents and primary caregivers can affect a child's development for good or ill.

Because the existing literature on child development was dominated at that time by approaches emphasizing physical and intellectual milestones, the Greenspans's book offered an important perspective, presenting observable behaviors which signal appropriate emotional development at each stage. The authors did not feel that emotional growth would necessarily take care of itself as long as other aspects of a child's development were proceeding apace, but that it deserved attention in and of itself.

The Greenspans presented six emotional milestones from birth to age four, noting that the times overlap because "there is great variability in a child's mastery of a particular stage and also to indicate the simultaneity of the course of the milestones" (Greenspan & Greenspan, 1985, 4).

0–3 months: Self-Regulation and Interest in the World
2–7 months: Falling in Love
3–10 months: Developing Intentional Communication
9–18 months: The Emergence of an Organized Sense of Self
18–36 months: Creating Emotional Ideas
30–48 months: Emotional Thinking

In his later book, *The Growth of the Mind* (1997), Greenspan revisits these same six stages and further develops each one, supporting and illustrating the thesis of his book: that "emotions, not cognitive stimulation, serve as the mind's primary architect" and that "the mind's highest capacities: intelligence, morality, and sense of self" (Greenspan, 1997, 1) share common origins in emotional experience.

The first milestone (0–3 months) is the gradual attainment of the feeling state that might be described as "calm interest." This state may last only a few minutes at a time in the first weeks of a baby's life, but it gradually lengthens as the infant learns the interplay of self-regulation and sensory experience. Focusing the senses on something in the environment helps the baby calm him- or herself down, and being calm allows the baby to take in more of the world through the senses. By the simple act of helping to settle a fussy baby, the parents are laying the foundation for the child's and future adult's ability to follow an experience of internal disharmony with calmness and attention, which then enables the person to focus creatively on whatever challenge is at hand. It also fosters the development of openness to a full range of sensory experiences without fear of being overwhelmed.

The second feeling milestone (2–7 months) is falling in love. The baby has used his or her ability gained from the previous stage, calm attention, to focus on one human person and to engage in real interaction. The parents' role is literally to "woo" the infant and provide him or her with a first experience of relationship. This entails encouraging a wide range of rich, deep feelings and behaviors, not unlike those experienced in courtship—special looks, mutual smiles and non-verbal sounds, awareness of each other's presence, and delight in physical closeness.

Out of this first immersion in delirious relationship sprouts a sense of shared humanity that can later blossom into the capacity to feel empathy and love. . . .

Without some degree of this ecstatic wooing by at least one adult who adores her, a child may never know the powerful intoxication of human closeness, never abandon herself to the magnetic pull of human relationships, never see other people as full human beings like herself, capable of feeling what she feels. (Greenspan, 1997, 50–51)

The infant now exists in relationship. Through emotional experience the baby has discerned the difference between inanimate and human presences and been invited through the parents' love into the human community. Greenspan suggests that while the infant is experiencing many positive feelings in being loved and cared for, it is not long before what is passively received turns to active, if brief, concern for others—caregivers, siblings, and eventually those beyond the family circle. The opposite developmental pathway is one that leads to isolation, false independence, "an unfeeling, self-centered, aggressive individual who can inflict injury without qualm or remorse" (Greenspan, 1997, 51).

The third milestone (3–10 months), developing intentional communication, is rooted in an infant's experience of being responded to via smiles, sounds, or gestures. This lets the baby know that his or her feelings and actions make a difference and that he or she is capable of eliciting a response from the most important people in the world. As the caregiver continues to respond emotionally in predictable ways, the infant begins to have a sense of a meaningful emotional world, far more important than learning that pulling a string on a toy will make a sound. The baby experiences a self that has desires, that those desires can be expressed, and that they can be affirmed by appropriate responses from the parents. Greenspan calls this "affective causality" (Greenspan, 1997, 37) and sees it as the root of any later ability to understand causality in more abstract and symbolic ways. The experience of affective causality fosters in the infant a sense of intentionality. A baby is "not born knowing he can cause something to happen; he must be taught by . . . reciprocation of his emotional responses" (Greenspan & Greenspan, 1985, 63).

The child is also learning at this stage how to be the receiving partner in an emotional dialogue and thus to engage in interactive communication. An infant gradually realizes that not all intentions and desires are mirrored and comes to experience a sense of separateness, the I and the one beyond the I: ". . . an outer reality, distinct from themselves and not always subject to their will, lies beyond their own feelings and desires" (Greenspan, 1997, 55). The toddler first learns what the adult must rely on throughout life, "how to send and receive the nonverbal messages that define both the boundaries that separate individuals and the common ground that lies between them" (Greenspan, 1997, 57).

The fourth milestone (9–18 months), the development of the organized sense of self, applies not only to the amazing burst of locomotive behaviors at this age, but also to emotive behaviors. It is not difficult to overlook growing complexity in the affective area because crawling, standing, and walking are so dramatic. But just as long chains of discrete units can be combined to produce unified movement, so too can long chains of discrete emotions be combined. And the two realms can be interwoven to produce complex sequences of emotion behaviors, which may be thought of as age-appropriate "actings out." There is a healthy link between what the baby is feeling and what the baby does. In the presence of an attentive caregiver, these emotion-behavior sequences have all the characteristics of a dramatic plot—conflict, climax, and denouement—performed Marcel Marceau style, without words. "The solid achievement of the fourth stage is the coalescence of larger and larger parts of the self through the bringing together of many intentions and affects. This organization arises in action" (Greenspan, 1997, 69–70). It is very important that caregivers can tolerate a wide range of feelings, that they stay with the child in order to work through the chain of emotions and help the child regain a sense of calm. If caregivers resort to "time outs" and leave the child alone, he or she will not be able to work through the emotional cycle and achieve integration, but may instead couple feelings of anger with feelings of abandonment and emptiness. By 18 months, we can talk about the child as having a character structure, a personality, a way of dealing with the world, based on the child's uniqueness and his or her experience of innumerable interchanges with the other.

The fifth milestone (18–36 months), creating emotional ideas, involves a number of new skills for the child. "In their rudimentary form, ideas are the way one's mind combines one's experiences with an object— what one has felt, seen, heard, and touched—into a multisensory image. An object's sensory and emotional characteristics are integrated with its functions to form a mental picture" (Greenspan and Greenspan, 1997, 129).

Children of this age are able to have emotional images or ideas that help them, for example, to remember mother or father when she or he is not actually present. This is an especially valuable coping device for the child that results from physical maturation of the nervous system and richness of affective experience.

The child of this age is also able to begin connecting physical sensations with words and to name feelings, thus adding another option for dealing with internal emotion states. Not only can feelings be experienced physically, not only can they be acted out behaviorally, but they can be talked about. With language the child can convey needs and desires, as well as likes and dislikes. In a warm and close relationship just the expression of feelings is itself pleasurable and provides a way of discharging emotions and finding one's way back to the basic state of calmness.

Even before children learn a full range of emotion words, we can see them expressing emotional ideas in play: dependency and security with a doll or a stuffed animal; pleasure with a favorite toy; curiosity in hide-and-seek games; assertiveness in arranging their pretend world; protest and anger when things do not go their way. Caregivers can help children by entering into their worlds, validating the full range of their emotions and drawing them into simple conversation about them. "By gently but firmly helping the child to translate her impulses into images and then to transmit these images to the consciousness of another person, the parent teaches the child an attitude of reflection" (Greenspan, 1997, 81), which contributes to a deep sense of self.

The sixth milestone (30–48 months), emotional thinking, is the child's ability to manipulate the various emotional ideas he has experienced and forge connections among them. Just as a child learns "to combine blocks to make an original house, so he can combine emotional ideas" (Greenspan & Greenspan, 1985, 173).

As more and more connections are made, a denser network of consciousness develops. This allows time to become comprehensible and space to become orderly. The world is more predictable and dependable. Fantasy and reality can be distinguished and, if all goes well, the sense of reality becomes stronger. The child can distinguish between what is inside and what is outside, what belongs to her and what belongs to others, what is subjective and what is objective.

The child is more able than ever to regulate and control impulses because he can see a connection between what he does and what will happen. She may be experiencing more stable moods, either positive or negative, which last for hours instead of minutes. Children of this age are developing the ability to concentrate, plan, and work toward a goal. They have a concept of self and other, and an understanding of the relationship between ideas, actions, and their consequences. This positions them to be able "to tolerate frustration, persevere at a task, and anticipate accomplishment" (Greenspan & Greenspan, 1985, 178). With the attainment of the sixth milestone, the child is in a position to develop all aspects of his or her personality as fully as possible. With the continued help of loving adults who support the child's efforts to organize increasingly complex inner and outer worlds, the child grows toward full maturity as a whole person.

The Child in the Catechesis of the Good Shepherd Atrium

Those familiar with Montessori's philosophy will sense the connections among her "normalized child," the "secure child" of Bowlby, and Greenspan's child at the sixth level of emotional development. These are the children who take to the Catechesis of the Good Shepherd atrium naturally because they have been prepared for the environment by skilled and loving parents or caretakers. But others will need the prepared environment to help them reach security and appropriate levels of emotional development. We cannot think that just because parents are interested in their child's development or just because they are religious people, that they will automatically have had the emotional maturity themselves to parent a child in emotionally effective ways. The sheer amount of time spent with an infant and toddler, his helplessness, her colic or illness, his resemblance to someone disliked or feared, her homeliness, the needs of other children, marital problems, financial or job pressures—all of these can literally bring out the worst in parents, and render them emotionally unavailable to their children. The quality of the parenting the parents themselves received is probably the greatest single determining factor, however, because the expression "We cannot give what we do not have" is as true in the emotional and relational realms as it is in any other. We know from attachment research that about 50 percent of children fall into one of the insecure categories, and there is little reason to believe that the population of the atrium is any different.

A superficial reading of Montessori attributes to the child almost preternatural qualities, as if he or she moves through the stages of childhood automatically and is, at all times, a messenger of peace to the adult world. But another way of reading Montessori suggests that she knew that even the young child can be disordered and in need of healing. The Montessori prepared environment and all that takes place within it could be thought of as group therapy for the preschool set. In our atria, too, there will be children who are insecure, who respond with anxiety to new situations, who withdraw into their private worlds, who are completely unpredictable. There will be the child who cannot calm herself, the child who cannot look the catechist in the eye, the child who acts out with hitting or head-banging, the child who cannot pick up on social cues, the child who doesn't know where he ends and the other begins. There will be the child who cannot express any emotion words, the child who cannot complete even one full cycle of a work, the child who cannot talk in any kind of coherent way. There will be the joyless child, the discouraged child, the angry child, the fearful child, the defiant child. Far from being the bane of a catechist's work, these children are the exact ones most in need of the atrium and all that it has to offer.

The catechist can, by creating an ordered and predictable environment, by developing genuine inner serenity, and by moving in slow and fluid ways, invite an anxious, distracted child into a place of calm. This may last only a moment, but it is a beginning and can lengthen over time. The atrium voice and the atrium walk are helps toward inner calmness, and prayer times in the atrium are especially powerful opportunities for the child to feel the support and containment of the whole group.

The catechist can, by being in touch with his or her own emotionality, by being alive to all forms of intimacy, and by being deeply empathic, invite an aloof or avoidant child into an emotional engagement he or she has never known. It is true that catechists are only unworthy servants and mere stewards of the treasure, and that the central person to be experienced in the atrium is the Good Shepherd, but if that mindset causes them to withhold themselves emotionally at times when the child needs genuine contact, then the soil will not be well-prepared for the seeds of the Spirit. Beginning catechists can sometimes become very focused on the materials in the atrium, as if these will by themselves engage the young child. The truth of the matter is that sometimes they do, and sometimes they do not. When they do not, the catechist must use all her personal charm and be positively enticing in order to draw the disengaged child into the beginnings of relationship. This will provide for the child a secure place from which to venture into exploration. Of course, the ultimate encounter we are hoping to facilitate is the one with the Good Shepherd, and often that encounter is richest for those children who are most lonely and most troubled. If these children are opened up to the tender mercy of Jesus in the atrium setting, it is possible for them to see hints of that love in the outside environment, impoverished though it may be.

The catechist can, by expressing him- or herself in feeling terms, by including emotional content in the scripture reflections, and by helping the children put even their strong feelings into words, assist the child in becoming a partner in emotional dialogue, and ultimately in prayer. The scriptural and liturgical presentations are rich in affective tone and invite the involvement of the imagination in symbolic thinking. The child who "gets" that he or she is one of the Good Shepherd's own sheep is a child who has a sense of self and other, who grasps "affective causality" and who can enter into a meaningful relationship. The parables of the lost coin and the lost sheep help the child know he or she can tolerate strong negative feelings and ultimately regain the peace and security of being loved.

The catechist can, by setting up the prepared environment, by attending to it carefully, and by making it a living, evolving space, continuously invite the children into orderly sequences of behavior. The incomparable blend of predictability and spontaneity in an atrium are powerful incentives for the child to become fully involved. At first the child may appear to be flailing about, but the discerning eye of the catechist can see in the apparently random movements a basic direction toward meaningful activity. It is important that the catechist be present to a child who is frustrated with a work or who wants to take away someone else's materials, because working through these disruptions with a loving companion can promote emotional integration and support future independence.

The catechist can, by carefully observing children in their work time, by engaging them in dialogue about their drawings, and by being open to special conversations initiated by the child, help to foster the growth of consciousness and increased ability to express themselves. By inviting connections among scriptural stories, and associations between the atrium and the everyday world, the catechist is helping the child find pleasure in constructing larger and larger realities, and be initiated into a process of reflection. By choosing music that integrates emotional and religious language, the catechist can support the child's deep understanding of herself, others, and God. And finally, when the child is "normalized," secure in his place in the atrium, and moving toward integration of feeling, thought, and action, the catechist can sit still on his or her small chair and observe the drama of each child, moving through ordered actions exuding the joy of a child of God.

These reflections are not meant to reduce what happens in the atrium to psychological development, but only to show that God's healing grace is needed for even the young child, who may have already experienced dark nights of the soul by the time she comes to us. They also underscore the wonderful work of Sofia Cavalletti and Gianna Gobbi, who have shown us what is possible in the atrium and the transformations that can occur. A child can literally be reborn and progress through any missed developmental stages in the safety of the atrium. The catechist is the witness of this amazing grace: to see a child rest securely in the arms of the Good Shepherd.

References

Ainsworth, M., and B. Wittig (1969). "Attachment and Exploratory Behaviour of One-year-olds in a Strange Situation." In B. M. Foss, ed., *Determinants of Infant Behavior* (pp. 111–36). London: Methuen.

Ainsworth, M. (1967). *Infancy in Uganda: Infant Care and the Growth of Love.* Baltimore: John Hopkins University Press.

Bartholomew, K. (1993). From childhood to adult relationships: Attachment theory and research. In S. Duck, ed., *Learning about Relationships* (pp. 30–62).

Bowlby, J. (1952/1965). *Child Care and the Growth of Love.* Harmondworth: Penguin.

———. (1969/1982). *Attachment.* New York: Basic Books.

———. (1973). *Separation: Anxiety and Anger.* New York: Basic Books.

———. (1979). *The Making and Breaking of Affectional Bonds:* New York: Routledge.

———. (1980). *Loss: Sadness and Depression.* New York: Basic Books.

———. (1988). *A Secure Base.* New York: Basic Books.

Brown, D. (1993). Affective development, psychopathology, and adaptation. In S. Ablon, D. Brown, E. Khantzian, and J. Mack, eds., *Human Feelings: Explorations in Affect Development and Meaning.* Hillsdale, NJ: The Analytic Press.

Greenspan, S., and N. Thorndike Greenspan (1985). *First Feelings: Milestones in the Emotional Development of Your Baby and Child.* New York: Penguin Books.

Greenspan, S. (1997). *The Growth of the Mind. Reading,* MA: Addison-Wesley Publishing Co., Inc.

Holmes, J. (1993). *John Bowlby and Attachment Theory:* New York: Routledge.

Kramer, G. (1992). A psychobiological theory of attachment. *Behavioral and Brain Sciences,* 15, 443–51.

Main, M., and J. Solomon (1986). "Discovery of an Insecure-disorganized/Disoriented Attachment Pattern." In T. B. Brazelton, M. W. Yogman, eds., *Affective Development in Infancy* (pp. 95–124). Norwood, NJ: Ablex Publishing.

Main, M., N. Kaplan, and J. Cassidy (1985). Security in infancy, childhood, and adulthood: A move to the level of representation. *Monographs of the Society for Research in Child Development,* 50, 66–104.

Shore, A. (1994). *Affect Regulation and the Origin of the Self.* Hillsdale, NJ: Lawrence Erlbaum Associates, Inc.

Stern, D. (1985). *The Interpersonal World of the Infant.* New York: Basic Books.

The Child: A Scriptural Image of the Holy Spirit

Francesca Cocchini

C hurch writers in the early Christian centuries interpreted a number of biblical passages as prefiguring the Holy Spirit, aptly illustrating his character and properties. One of them stands out—at least on first appraisal—as being alien to its pneumatologic framework. It is the text in Matthew 18:1–6 where Jesus places a child in the midst of the disciples, pointing him out as an example. The interpretation I refer to, and will go on to explain, is given by Origen, the great exegete and theologian from Alexandria who lived in the first half of the third century. According to Origen, the child "Jesus called and placed in their midst" represents the Holy Spirit. Now there is no doubt that the connection between Holy Spirit and child in the light of modern exegesis cannot but appear surprising, let alone fanciful; however, in the eyes of someone who for many years has witnessed the religious experience of children, it is extraordinarily realistic. Between children and the Holy Spirit there exists a close relationship so profound—one could say natural—that it leads us to believe that Origen's exegesis is not too arbitrary. It is therefore in homage to the Catechesis of the Good Shepherd—which enables us to discover more and more each day this "child" in God's eyes—that I present in these brief notes the suggestive and dense excerpt from Origen.

Origen is commenting on Matthew's Gospel and, regarding the passage of Matthew 18:1–6, he offers, as he usually does, more than one explanation. The first one is defined as of "simple meaning": it regards the immediate understanding of the passage that we gather from a literal reading. To the question, How is it possible to "become like a child"? Origen responds with a detailed description of what was, in his time, the common idea of a child: a being who has not yet experienced "sensual pleasures" and therefore enjoys freedom of the senses. He has not yet attained the full use of reason and hence is free from any excess of passion. Origen writes:

As, then, it has been accurately demonstrated also by others that no
passion affects little children who have not yet attained the full use of
reason; and if there is no passion, it is obvious there is neither any fear.
And, even if in children there is found something that resembles the
passions, they are faint, and very quickly suppressed . . . as, for example,
in the case of children there is a forgetfulness of evils at the very time
of their tears, for they change in a moment, and laugh and play along
with those who were thought to grieve and frighten them, but who
in truth had not brought about such emotions in them. So too, moreover,
one will humble oneself like the little child whom Jesus called (Matthew
18:4, 2); for neither haughtiness, nor conceit because of one's noble
birth, nor wealth, nor any of those things which are thought to be good,
but in reality are not so, comes to a little child. This is why you may
see children who at a very tender age, up to three or four, like those
who are of mean birth, though they may seem to be of noble birth, and
do not appear at all to love rich children rather than the poor.[1]

If this is the "child," it follows that Jesus' invitation to conversion and
to become like him means "to reach the point of having, so to speak, the
least degree of passions, as children have." And Origen concludes:

Therefore, if the disciples of Jesus accept, guided by reason, what
children experience simply based on their age, i.e., the overcoming of
those passions which exalt whoever is deprived of reason, they humble
themselves like the child that Jesus pointed out, not being exalted
because of vainglory, nor puffed up because of wealth or raiment, nor
elated because of noble birth.[2]

Besides, already in another work, Origen had interpreted Jesus' invitation in an ethical sense, and his interpretation would be adopted in subsequent Christian tradition:

To exhort his followers to the "new birth" (John 3:5), Jesus says to
them: "Unless you turn and become like children, you will never enter
the kingdom of heaven" (Matthew 18:3). Notice the precise expression.
Children do not take revenge on those who do them harm; they do
not become sad over the loss of pleasures; they do not become firmly
attached to flattery. Therefore, Jesus wants us to become by our frame

of mind what children are by age. They are not so by reason, but others *are* because they become so by following Jesus' commandment and doing their best with reason and with habits in order to be like that.[3]

But Origen, as we said, is not content with the first interpretation. He therefore goes on to propose a second one, which he presents "by way of teaching and practical instruction." This is a formula that recurs often in the exegetic writings of the Alexandrian teacher. It denotes both the scholastic climate enveloping the study of scripture, characterized by an ongoing concern to pose problems and find solutions for them, and the inexhaustible depth of meaning that he attributed to the sacred texts, for which many interpretative solutions could be advanced but could never be deemed definitive. In line with time-honored Judaic hermeneutics, Origen believes that the Word of God is refracted into many rays, and the interpreter's task is to discover them through ceaseless research. In this case, however, the fullness of Origen's argument to explain his second proposed interpretation leads me to believe that he considers it not only valid but actually the only one possible.

Also, Origen's method for penetrating the deepest meaning of a certain passage beneath the literal meaning is taken from Judaic exegetic practice. It consists in putting next to the passage in question another passage, linked to it by the presence of a similar term. In our case, the term is *child* and the passage Origen puts next to Matthew 18:2 is Isaiah 8:18 where the Lord says, "Here I am with the children the Lord has given me." But let us follow the commentary. First of all, Origen asks just who is the "child put in their midst," or "put in the rational mind of the disciples." And he immediately gives the answer. It is the Holy Spirit, who, "descended from His own perfection to humankind, was called and placed by Jesus in the midst of the disciples." In fact, the Holy Spirit "made Himself small for the salvation of humankind" and was "placed by Jesus in the mind of the disciples" to be imitated by them. It follows that the invitation to "become small like this child means to become like the Holy Spirit," so that the Savior may pronounce the words placed in his mouth by Isaiah 8:18: "Here I am with the children the Lord has given me." In fact, these "children" who enter the kingdom of heaven are those who "have turned away from the affairs of the world" and have become bearers of the Holy Spirit.

Aware of the boldness of his proposed interpretation, Origen seeks another confirmation of it. He finds it by comparing the last expression of the text, "Whoever receives one of these children in my name receives me" (Matthew 18:5), with the parallel text from Luke, which says, "Whoever receives this child in my name receives me" (Luke 9:48). Luke's variant— "this child" instead of "one of these children"—is not insignificant. Origen notes that Jesus did not invite the disciples to receive children in general, but one particular individual, i.e., "this child," the one "whom Jesus took and placed by His side." This is a precision that, as he points out, makes it necessary to interpret the passage figuratively, so it applies to every one of the faithful. As Origen explains, "It is necessary that this child, whom Jesus took and placed by His side, be received by each one of us in the name of Jesus." But it is only the Holy Spirit who "lives as an immortal Being," enabling everyone, at all times and everywhere, to "receive him in the name of Jesus from Jesus Himself." "And Jesus," continues Origen in explaining the words of the promise, "does not distance Himself. He comes to the one who receives the child, so that it is accordingly said: 'Whoever receives this child in my name receives me.'"

Origen introduces Luke's text to confirm the pneumatologic interpretation he had proposed for Matthew's passage. From this he continues to analyze Luke's text and he notices another expression where mention is made of the child (Luke 18:17): "If anyone does not receive the kingdom of God like a child, he or she will never enter it." In this case, too, Origen proposes an explanation. He points out the twofold meaning of the term *child:* it refers to whoever receives the kingdom or to the kingdom itself. This is how he explains it:

> The expression can have a double meaning: Either those who receive the kingdom of God become like little children, or they receive the kingdom of God which for them has become like a little child. And perhaps those who receive the kingdom of heaven here on earth receive it as though this kingdom were a child, whereas in the future world they will no longer receive it as such, but according to the perfection of their spiritual maturity, so to speak, which perfection is manifested to all those who in the present time receive it, when it is here as a little child.

It is evident that Origen prefers the second interpretative possibility, which is also the more difficult one: It is the kingdom that Jesus presents "like a child."

Once again there is an equivalency that modern exegesis would surely deem arbitrary and fanciful. However, for one who is accustomed to meditating with children on the history of the kingdom, it is an extraordinarily appropriate interpretation. In fact, when children meditate on the kingdom, they usually stress above all its growth, placing it alongside the parallel of the mustard seed, "which is the smallest of all seeds, but becomes the biggest of all plants." Perhaps, as Origen suggests, this happens because children feel that the reality of the kingdom is very much like their own reality. Kingdom and child are both realities tending toward the perfection of the *parousia,* infused with the same force that makes them "grow" like the seed, like the yeast.

Translated by Father Joseph Occhio, SDB

Notes

1. *Com. Matthew 13:16.* Most of this English text is taken from "The Ante-Nicene Fathers," ed. Allan Menzies, vol. X, Wm. B. Eerdmans Publishing Company, Michigan, 1969, pp. 484–87.

2. Ibid.

3. *Com. John Fr. 3:5.*

Reflections of Some Former Children of Sofia's and Gianna's Atrium

Why is it that I wanted my children to attend this catechesis center as I had? From the thought of eternity and from our faith, the way is short to the spiritual place where we learned about these realities, the Maria Montessori Center of Catechesis, which came to mind with a sweet reminiscence. This indeed is a motivation.

Besides this background, there are more precise reasons at the root of the choice (shared, of course, by my wife). My remembrance of the center is truly a good one. All parents want their children to go through their own positive experiences.

Another reason is the desire that our children's religious experience and reflection have a well-defined and important place. At this center, I experienced for the first time the effort made to understand difficult concepts or hidden truths (for instance, through a study of the parables); hence, I learned to associate faith with the exercise of thinking. Naturally, I hope this will happen all over again with my children.

Another reason is the realization that our Catholic faith is in some respects simple, but in others complex. It also has a development, which, in part, is unavoidably institutionalized. A conscious, personal orientation makes dialogue possible and therefore a relationship with the Church stable.

A further reason lies in the fact that the center assures the children a religious experience independent from the other institutions in which they are, or will be, included (family, school, work, community, and so forth), which keeps the faith safe from any future contention over those institutions.

Lastly, there is a consideration of a general nature that also matters greatly: The development of one's spiritual life and the attainment of conscious orientations, austere as they may be, are sources of serenity also from the human standpoint. Their absence does not bring joyous freedom, but rather most often just tentatives of liberation from boring coercions caused by everyday human habits.

Felice Ancora

My strongest recollection, the most vivid one I have, is of the day I wrote my name in request to receive first Communion (I had just begun first grade!) on that small white card that ended up, with all the other cards, in the small first Communion case. I felt little, and yet the call of love was big and strong. I experienced only a great peace, because that Good Shepherd was truly special ("Even though I walk through the darkest valley, I fear no evil; for you are with me") and he would lead me to drink water and would bring me to pasture in green valleys. I had found joy, safety, and the awareness that he would never abandon me!

I wish to thank Sofia and Gianna, the shining presences of my childhood, for everything they gave to us who were children at the time, and for everything they give to the children of today: mustard seeds that will spring up also tomorrow.

Sofia Barchiesi

I liked above all to mix the yeast with the flour and water and to think about what would then happen. You couldn't do it too often because it made a mess.

I remember also the reddish light of the small stove and the cloth-covered mixture that would leaven . . . a mystery. And you had to wait.

And then the pearl, the mystery of beauty, I remember well. It seemed easy at the time to realize which was the most beautiful pearl, and to understand the reasons why the merchant exchanged the little ones for the big one. It was only natural, even if now at times the memory, clouded by the need to do things (typical of adults), becomes doubtful with certain choices made in life: Should you give away all the little pearls? At the time, it was the one beauty, and the rest . . . the only natural response to beauty. Now the pearl remains for me as the image of God's kingdom as hope; and it is no small thing.

It isn't strange that my idea of the Church has more to do with the people of God than with the hierarchy! Every once in a while, during a sermon, the image of the sheep without a shepherd becomes painful, and I think of the kind face of the shepherd made of wood that I used to work with as a little girl; and I realize that, all things considered, there is only one shepherd.

Anna Aluffi Pentini

For a number of years I went to the Montessori School of Religion (that was the name they gave it then), from the time I was five or six years old up until I was fourteen and perhaps even beyond. My recollection of those years is bound up in certain sensations that reappear in jumbled order: first of all, the environment, the unusual atmosphere of the gigantic apartment that served as a school, an old house, decidedly serious and austere, above all when compared with the Montessori elementary school I attended at the time. I recall the colors that tended to be dark amid a lot of polished wood that added to the seriousness of the environment. I remember well the three flights of stairs, with the last flight having steps that were higher and harder to climb. Especially when I was smaller, reaching the school was always a minor conquest.

I recall my fascination over the various small models and card materials spread throughout the school. Today I seem to find a natural connection between the environment's "antiquated scenery" and the materials that helped us children to enter actively into the atmosphere of events that occurred in such a long-past period of history. More than anything, I recall the sheepfold and the sheep of the Good Shepherd and the stone removed from the empty tomb of Jesus.

But besides the environment, what helped the most to create a special atmosphere was the total attention given at any time to every word and every thought expressed by us children. It was an attention I found nowhere else with the same intensity. This strong attention was very perceptible. And if, on the one hand, it taught us to give value and importance to the expression of our emotions and to the way of expressing them, on the other hand it could make the more timid children perhaps consider their words a little too carefully. (At times, I chose not to speak.)

Today I am left with a positive and distinct memory of those years, as of a world set apart: the sensation of having drawn close to religion in a privileged (and perhaps a little elitist) way and of having had the opportunity to reflect on and to be "educated" to explore the words of the Gospel and the Bible, taking all the time you needed and, perhaps, expanding on them somewhat.

Four years ago, I had the occasion to bring my children to the same center. It was delightful to see how after 25 years nothing, but nothing, had changed. And all the more do I think how the children of today, the boys and girls of a world that runs without thinking anymore, should be grateful to people who teach them to stop, to reflect all together, and to understand

and interiorize such great and essential themes, like the presence of God and the Christian message.

Giuseppe Hirsch

They were beautiful times, which I now recall with nostalgia. The time we spent on the parables was very interesting. When we came together, it was really nice to think quietly and to discuss things among ourselves.

Daniele

Sofia was good at explaining things, and the voice of the catechist was inviting.

Maria Neve

Sofia would give us a warm welcome.

Maria Elena

When we arrived, she greeted us with a handshake.

Daniele

It was very enjoyable to go where I had a lot of things to do.

Maria Elena

My brother and I used to look forward with joy to Wednesday and we often would ask, "When are we going to Sofia's?" We would get ready early in the morning, choosing the most beautiful clothes. We ran up the stairs of Sofia's building, trying to imagine the afternoon's activities.

   When I entered for the first time that "room of the older ones" (ages 6 –9), my attention was immediately drawn by something I had never seen before: history. Yes, the "strip of the history of the kingdom of God," which, beginning with creation, unraveled calmly on the walls of the room until it reached our present day and even beyond, to the *parousia*. Finally, "time" had a spatial dimension; I could almost touch it. It seems I always wanted to see time in that new way and I stopped to look at the painted strip, trying to grasp as many images as possible.

In all the years that followed, the "strip of history" was a key point of reference. Even now, when I study, I go over in my mind, as far as possible, the entire past to understand better the present. As I look back on it now, it seems that I have received time as a gift, and it is a very big gift for a child! But time alone is not sufficient for us to understand humans, and humans alone are not sufficient to make history. At the Center of Catechesis we searched for answers to this very problem. It is the theme that accompanied me in my infancy up until first Communion and in my adolescence up until Confirmation. Even now I haven't found a solution. But perhaps the solution lies in continuing to search.

Benedetta Albani

It is hard to put in a few words what the atrium of Sofia Cavalletti and Gianna Gobbi means to me, because I would need categories not found in the practical structure of language.

There I encountered and always will encounter the Good Shepherd, and there, in a special way, I have lived this encounter as a thing most natural and serene, almost instinctive.

This possibility of encounter is a treasure I hope to cherish always and to tell others about.

Filippo Calabresi, an "ex-bambino" *who, thanks to the experience of the Catechesis of the Good Shepherd, is still somewhat of a child.*

Words of a Former Atrium Child at the Funeral of Gianna Gobbi

I remember Gianna at Via degli Orsini when I was a child. We always addressed her in a familiar way by her first name, without any shyness. I loved her without knowing why; I understood more when I was happy to meet her again because of my children. I understood that she was capable of watching children attentively, without letting them notice it, without being always on their back.

Gianna listened to children attentively, letting them be fully children; she smiled like a little girl, but she took them quite seriously with the intelligence of the mind and of the heart. She was capable of going straight to the point; she never avoided her task as an adult who is an educator. She used very precise words with the children and for the children, and with us, the parents, when speaking about our children.

In my remembrance it seems as if Gianna's task would be to take the children by the hand and bring them to the Word of God, and as if Sofia's task would be to bring the Word of God to the children. This complementarity made possible the encounter with the Good Shepherd, the amazement in front of the pearl, the leaven, the hidden treasure, the mystery of the kingdom of heaven.

When I was a child I do not remember having said goodbye to her, because at a certain moment she discreetly disappeared. Not even now do I say goodbye, but the spontaneity with which we met again makes me think that also in the future it will be the same.

Thank you, Gianna, rest in peace and wait for us, the ones who from time to time, like some of "your children," still ask, "But what is it like, this kingdom of heaven?"

Anna Aluffi Pentini

Some Statements from Former Atrium Children, Now Adults between 40 and 50 Years Old, at a Reunion in the Atrium

The pearl, the vine, the sheepfold, the light, the coins, the yeast, and so forth—all these things helped to confirm in me the certainty that the Lord speaks to me in confidence and knows me and really calls me by name.

[The Catechesis] taught us to ask ourselves questions about life, and this was very important.

Thank you for the education in freedom I received from this center, for the deep sense of spirituality you evoked, which enabled me to want to and know how to meditate on and confront the essential experiences of life as though writing a poem, having always with me a serene sense of mystery.

In recalling the long period spent outside the life of faith, I said that what always lingered with me of the period spent in here was the fact of having received and lived very important things.

What really made a mark on us here is the fact that we can only be satisfied with great things.

The great joy is to see that what we remember here is not something over and done with, but something that still goes on and is alive, both in us and here. In this place there was an atmosphere that was all prayer.

We felt a curiosity in the positive sense of the word, and openness toward others; and this I passed on to others.

We had the sense of doing something together with the adults, a continual discovery made together.

We breathed an atmosphere of great freedom.

We learned to ask ourselves questions about life.

The parables were a sheer delight. About the parables, I remember the questions, the search for answers, and, at times, the flashes of inspiration when an answer came from out of the blue and was just blurted out as it were.

Among the most vivid recollections, there is certainly the lesson of silence.

Our atrium was for us a place of the soul.

Translated by Father Joseph Occhio, SDB

Contributors

Luigi C. Capogrossi has known and worked with the Catechesis of the Good Shepherd since its beginnings. He is President of the Maria Montessori Association for the Religious Formation of Children.

Sofia Cavalletti is a Hebrew Scripture scholar who has devoted the past 50 years to the religious formation of children. The Catechesis of the Good Shepherd, as this approach is known, has spread to countries around the world.

Francesca Cocchini is a professor of the history of Christianity in the Faculty of Letters and Philosophy of the University of G. d'Annunzio of Chieti. Formerly she was a researcher in the Department of Historic-Religious Study, Faculty of Letters and Philosophy of the University of La Sapienza in Rome.

Patrizia Cocchini is a catechist in Rome. She is also a medical doctor with specialization in pediatrics, neonatology, and preventive medicine.

Patricia M. Coulter has worked full time in the ministry of the Catechesis of the Good Shepherd since her training in Rome in 1977. She has been the director of the Catechesis of the Good Shepherd for the Archdiocese of Toronto since 1987, and the director of the Catechesis of the Good Shepherd certificate program at the University of St. Michael's College, University of Toronto since 1991. She is a co-author of *The Good Shepherd and the Child: A Joyful Journey.*

Brother Ignatius J. Feaver, OFM CAP, is a spiritual director and Director of the Franciscan Internship Program for Spiritual Direction. He has worked in faith formation for educators and as an instructor in spiritual direction at Regis College, Toronto, Canada.

David Kahn, is Director of the North American Montessori Teachers Association and editor of the *NAMTA Journal.* He is the founding director of Hershey Montessori Farm School in Concord, Ohio, and teaching principal at Ruffing Montessori School in Rocky River, Ohio.

Tina Lillig is the national director of the Catechesis of the Good Shepherd Association (USA). She has been a catechist of the Good Shepherd for 25 years. Her book, *The Catechesis of the Good Shepherd in the Parish Setting* (LTP) was published in 1998.

Dalmazio Mongillo, OP, is a professor of moral theology and president of the Ecumenical Institute of St. Nicholas di Bari. He has been a friend and advisor to the Catechesis for many years.

Silvana Quattrocchi Montanaro received her degree in medicine and surgery, with a specialty in psychiatry from the University of Rome. Presently she is a teaching professor of postgraduate medical doctors and psychologists. She is also the Director of Training in the Association Montessori Internationale (AMI) course for assistants to infancy. Among her published works are *Understanding the Human Being* and *The Child Is the Father of the Man.* She is a co-author of *The Good Shepherd and the Child: A Joyful Journey.*

Lupita Palafox has been a catechist since 1976. She studied with Sofia in Mexico and in Rome where she also studied the Montessori method. Currently she is a consultant to the Catechesis in Mexico.

Rebekah Rojcewicz is a catechist and formation leader in the Catechesis of the Good Shepherd in the United States and director of the Good Shepherd Center in Memphis, Tennessee. She studied with Sofia and Gianna at the Centro di Catechesi in Rome from 1979 to 1981 and has served on the International Council since 1996. Rebekah has translated several of Sofia's books and articles into English, including *The Religious Potential of the Child 6 to 12 Years Old.*

Barbara Schmich Searle is a counseling psychologist in South Bend, Indiana. She has been a catechist at all three levels of the Catechesis of the Good Shepherd, as well as an artist and liturgist at the Notre Dame Center for Liturgy in Notre Dame, Indiana.